PERRY

Identify Prophetic Triggers That Lead to the Rapture and Great Tribulation

PROPHETIC ALERT

Stunning New Insights Reveal What's Coming Soon!

Prophetic Alert: Stunning New Insights Reveal What's Coming Soon!

Published by Voice of Evangelism Ministries
P. O. Box 3595
Cleveland TN 37320
423.478.3456
www.perrystone.org

This book or parts thereof may not be reproduced in any form, stored in a retrieval system, or transmitted in any form by any means—electronic, mechanical, photocopy, recording, Internet, or otherwise—without prior written permission of the publisher, except as provided by United States of America copyright law.

Unmarked Scripture quotations are from the
King James Version of the Bible.

Scripture quotations marked NKJV are from the New Kings James Version of the Bible. Copyright © 1979, 1980, 1982 by Thomas Nelson, Inc., publishers. Used by permission.

First Edition © 2025

Printed in the United States of America

ISBN: 978-0-9895618-7-7

All rights reserved

Cover Design/Illustration & Layout: Michael Dutton

CONTENTS

1	One Major Event Can Trigger the Rapture and Tribulation	5
2	The Cain Spirit in the Lands East of Eden	9
3	Land of the Assassins and Gate of the Gods	17
4	Satan's Angelic Prince Spirits Ruling the Nations	23
5	A Cosmic Wrestling Match	33
6	Why Do Many Muslims Dislike the Jews and Israel?	41
7	Prophetic Visions of the Serpent of Gaza	51
8	When the Abyss Releases the Destroyers	61
9	The People of the Beast Meet the Lion in Bashan	67
10	God Versus Gog – Big Hooks in Little Jaws	75
11	Can the Antichrist Overtake a Militarily Armed Israel?	85
12	The Strongest Middle Eastern Prince Spirit on the Loose	93
13	The Prophetic Seven-year Treaty	105
14	Ezekiel's War and the Rapture Link	119
15	When a Dead Head Rises Again	127
16	The Confusion Over Who Is Gog of Magog	135
17	This Will Shock the World	147
18	God's Four Weapons of Destruction Are Coming	151
19	Kings of the East and 1.5 Billion Hindus	163
20	Does the Bible Hint of Nuclear War?	169

21	The Prophecy—When America Stops Protecting Israel	183
22	Five Ways a Nation Can Delay Judgment and Keep God's Favor	193
23	In Conclusion	207

CHAPTER 1

ONE MAJOR EVENT CAN TRIGGER THE RAPTURE AND TRIBULATION

Current global events are causing people around the world, including non-believers, to ask themselves: *Are we entering the time of the end?* From people who are well-versed in biblical end-time topics, to the unsaved person who has heard a few things here and there, people have a growing awareness that the chaos we're seeing around the world could be a sign of prophetic end-time events.

I have been asked on numerous occasions; *"What is the greatest trigger that will lead to the Rapture of the church and the Great Tribulation?"* This book will search for answers to this recurring question as we examine forthcoming events, sometimes from a different perspective.

In hindsight, we see evidence that single major events occurring at a significant time had the capacity to alter the course of history, sometimes not just for nations, but for the world. We watch history seemingly repeating itself, as Ecclesiastes 1:9 tells us, "That which has been is what will be, that which is done is what will be done, and there is nothing new under the sun."

Christ spoke about the days of Noah and Lot, pointing to the fact that people who lived during the times of both men had not the faintest notion of what was about to unfold. They were unaware until *the day* that the deluge of water overwhelmed and drowned them, and the hot fire and brimstone rained from heaven and burned Sodom and Gomorrah to ashes (Matt. 24:36-39). The flood altered the course of human history, and the destruction of four cities by the Dead Sea changed the geographical landscape. We could say the same is true today.

There are circumstances and global events that I refer to as *prophetic triggers*. God uses these to seize the attention of His people and the world, sending them a message to indicate that the words He spoke that were penned in ancient biblical prophecies are beginning to occur. As these signs and signals unfold, we witness the release of a new awareness of Almighty God, His written prophetic messages, and warnings designed to refocus the eyes, minds, and spirits of those who can properly discern and interpret these events. Often this leads to the awareness of the need to repent and turn to God.

When Hitler rose to prominence as chancellor of Germany, his horrible twelve years of Jewish persecution, culminating in the deadly Holocaust, triggered an important prophetic event: the nation of Israel was reborn in a day (Isa. 66:8). This sudden and dramatic fulfillment of prophecy triggered a renewal in the message of Christ's return. It stirred a restoration revival that set ablaze America and parts of the world, as it focused on the miraculous works of God.

On May 14th, 1948, David Ben-Gurion announced to the world the establishment of a Jewish homeland called the State of Israel. Within hours, war was declared by Arabs in surrounding countries. An event that should have led to a time of rejoicing for the Jews and survivors of the horrible Holocaust instead led to months of the infant nation battling for its very survival.

ONE MAJOR EVENT CAN TRIGGER THE RAPTURE AND TRIBULATION

Statehood of Israel was a prophetic trigger. Based on Old Testament prophecies, the return of the Messiah would not and could not happen until Israel was again in possession of the original land given to Abraham's offspring, and until the city of Jerusalem was united—another trigger that happened in the 1967 Six-Day War (Psa. 102:16).

This book will feature new insights and interesting details about a major event that was prophesied over 2,500 years ago and will unfold in Israel, leading to the return of Christ and the coming tribulation. We will delve into the involvement of prince spirits and the angels over Israel. A chapter is included that uses biblical evidence that appears to indicate the future use of nuclear weapons. The book includes information on:

- the ancient spirit of Cain and the connection to Iran (Persia) and terrorism;

- the strong prince spirit that is controlling the Middle East—the prince over Persia;

- how the Antichrist might successfully invade Israel, despite their great army and military resources;

- the timing of the war of Gog of Magog, with new details gleaned from the Hebrew text;

- the hook that God could use to bring Islamic nations into a war of their own destruction;

- one reason some Muslims hate the Jews, based on a little-known, centuries old event;

- the vision of the serpent of Gaza and the Gaza War;

- when the abyss releases the destroyer.

This book will explain the Ezekiel trigger—the one upcoming major event that will unleash the final signs of the birth pains of the Messiah and His return!

Note: Throughout this book, I will use both Iran and Persia, the biblical name, to identify the nation of Iran.

CHAPTER 2

THE CAIN SPIRIT IN THE LANDS EAST OF EDEN

"And Cain went out from the presence of the Lord, and dwelt in the land of Nod, on the east of Eden" (Genesis 4:16 KJV).

The story begins with Cain and his early lineage. To correctly interpret end-time prophecy, including past and future wars between Israel and her enemies, one must understand that these clashes are not about political jockeying for land. They are spiritually charged, and they involve competing and conflicting religious beliefs, with each group locked into their own apocalyptic ideologies.

We must also understand how regions such as Iran, Afghanistan, Pakistan, Iraq, and Syria became breeding grounds for hatred toward Israel and the Jews. Behind this motivation for Israel's destruction are ancient prince spirits that have controlled or influenced the leaders of these nations since ancient times. In the last days, these ancient spirits will rise and work through leaders to forge history's final and most dangerous military and economic coalitions. The final wars of prophecy will be waged on a world stage where the first cities took shape, in the land of the wanderings of Cain and his descendants.

THE CRADLE OF CIVILIZATION

Genesis 2:10-14 lists four rivers that formed the eastern and western boundaries of the famed Garden of Eden, man's first home. The rivers are listed as Pishon, Gihon, Tigris (Hiddekel in some translations), and Euphrates. The land mass within the boundaries of these four rivers encompasses an area of about 1,500 square miles and is known as the Cradle of Civilization. The earliest name was Mesopotamia, an ancient Greek word meaning "between the rivers."

The land around the Tigris and Euphrates Rivers became the earliest centers for farming, thus giving the region another title, the Fertile Crescent. According to Genesis, the Tigris and Euphrates are the eastern rivers that bordered the biblical Garden of Eden. The headwaters of both rivers begin in eastern Turkey and flow south, eventually emptying into the Persian Gulf. The Euphrates is presently the main water source in Turkey, Syria, and Iraq.

The far western river of Eden is the Gihon, which is the Nile River, according to the Jewish historian Josephus. He said the Greeks called it the Nile:

> "...and Geon [Gihon] runs through Egypt, and denotes what arises from the east, which the Greeks call Nile."
> – Josephus: Antiquities, Book I, chapter 1, part 3

Josephus' statement aligns with scripture, which indicates the Gihon flows around "the whole land of Ethiopia" (Gen. 2:13). The Nile begins there and flows northward toward Egypt.

The land of Ethiopia was the land of Cush, the son of Noah's son Ham (Gen. 10:6) and is marked on old maps as the region of Northern Africa, including Ethiopia, Sudan, and Egypt. The earliest scholars believed that the Ethiopians were descendants of Cush.

Numerous theories attempt to identify the fourth river, the Pishon.

Moses wrote that this river flowed through the land of Havilah where there was gold (Gen. 2:11). This serves as a clue to identify the area of the Pishon River. The land of Havilah (according to older scholarly maps) is the region of the Arabian Peninsula. Notice this commentary:

> "Bochart places it (the Pishon) in the southeastern part of Arabia, not far from the Persian Gulf (cf. Gen 10:7, 29) where a large district of that name is mentioned as divided between two different tribes of Shemites and of Hamites, deriving Havilah from a Hebrew root which signifies sand, its sandy character being probably the origin of its designation."
>
> – JAMIESON, FAUSSET, AND BROWN COMMENTARY

Many historical writers believe the land of Havila was in the region of Saudi Arabia. With the Arabian Peninsula being mostly sandy and dry, what happened to this river that once flowed through the land of Eden? Author James Sauer released information in Biblical Archeology Review Magazine (July/August 1996) in which he examined satellite imagery taken over Saudi Arabia. The satellite revealed a jagged seam of limestone rock that was once part of a river channel but now was covered by sand dunes. An ancient river once cut across the Arabian Peninsula, and Mr. Sauer suggests that this river may be the Pishon River associated with one of the four rivers of Eden. The river dried up between 3500 and 2000 BC. Prior to that, evidence shows that the region was much wetter.

The Pishon flowed around Havilah where there is gold and precious stones (Gen. 2:10-12). There are numerous areas on the Arabian Peninsula where gold and precious stones would have been mined, one of which is Mahd edh-Dhahab. The mine is 125 miles south of Medina, near the headwaters of the river believed to be the biblical Pishon.

Some have theorized that this ancient gold mine in western Saudi Arabia, located near the biblical city of Ophir, was King Solomon's mine. This would align with 1 Kings 9:26-28, which tells us that King Solomon built a fleet of ships in Ezion-geber, near Eloth on the shore of the Red Sea, and servants and sailors went to Ophir and brought back four hundred and twenty talents of gold.

The gold mining history at Mahd edh-Dhahab dates back 3,000 years, meaning that it was actively mined in biblical times. An American geologist located and identified the mine in 1932, and Saudi Arabia reactivated the mining site in 1988. It isn't possible to say exactly how much gold was mined here in ancient times, but estimates vary from one to five metric tons. The fact that this gold mine is located adjacent to the dried riverbed adds further to the suggestion that this was once a location of the Pishon River of Eden.

Research of these four rivers has helped us identify their locations:

- The Euphrates flows through Turkey, Syria, and Iraq.
- The Hiddekel (Tigris) flows through Turkey, Syria, and Iraq.
- The Gihon (Nile), the longest river in Africa and one of the longest in the world, fans out into the fertile Nile Delta and empties into the Mediterranean Sea on the coast of Egypt.
- The Pishon was once in Arabia but is now a dried riverbed covered with sand.

CAIN AND THE BOUNDARIES OF EDEN

Looking at the headwaters of the four rivers and following the flow of the rivers of Eden, we can see how the land of Eden was not just a small garden in Adam's backyard. The beautiful garden would have extended from the Nile in the west to the Tigris River in Iraq in the

THE CAIN SPIRIT IN THE LANDS EAST OF EDEN

East. Within the boundaries of these rivers, Adam and Eve lived in Eden, and human life on Earth began.

After Adam and Eve were banished from Eden, two sons, Cain and Abel, were born. In a footnote, the historian Josephus mentions that thirty-three sons and twenty-three daughters were born to Adam and Eve after the fall. As an adult, Cain murdered his brother Abel after becoming jealous when God favored Abel's sacrifice above Cain's. Thus, the first murder is linked with *worship, religion, and sacrifices.*

The book of Jasher records that Cain killed Abel in a field using the iron blade of his plowing instrument (Jasher 1:26). After this, God placed a mark on Cain to protect him from future retaliation. After the murder, "Cain went out from the presence of the LORD and dwelt in the land of Nod, on the east of Eden." Nod comes from a Hebrew word that means "to flee, wander, or roam." Cain settled on the east of Eden (Gen. 4:16). Traveling past the easternmost boundary of the rivers of Eden, in this case the Hiddekel (Tigris), would bring Cain to a land mass that would one day become the nation of Persia, or as it is called today, Iran.

CAIN AND THE SPIRIT OF MURDER

This area east of Eden is also the territory where most modern terrorists are trained and terrorism activity is initiated or planned. It includes the area of the Shi'ite Muslims of Iran, the Taliban in Afghanistan, and the Islamic radicals in certain cities of Pakistan. In these three nations, sharia law is enforced, and within those groups an unknown number are prone to violence against others.

In early biblical history, note that the first ten generations from Adam to the flood lived long lives. In Genesis 5, before the flood, the average lifespan of the nine righteous men was 912 years. In the 1,656 years from Adam to the flood, with people living longer and having more children, the population could have been between several million to hundreds of millions. By Noah's time the earth was corrupt and filled with violence. All flesh had been corrupted by fallen angels who took on human form, reproduced with women, and procreated a race of giants (Gen. 6:4-12).

According to several early church fathers, as well as the book of Enoch, these fallen angels taught men to use weapons, and they promoted immoral behavior and violence. Both Jude 1:6-7 and 2 Peter 2:4 speaks of *fallen angels*. According to ancient beliefs, a group of angels were sent to the earth in the form of humans for the purpose of teaching people how to follow God. But they failed in their assignment.

After Adam and Eve were banished from the Garden, human population grew through their sons and daughters and Cain's lineage. This happened primarily east of Eden, around the Fertile Crescent, in the Mesopotamian region that was known in ancient times as Sumer, Akkad, Assyria, and Babylonia. Today these are the areas of Iraq, Syria, and Turkey.

As years passed, people began to engage excessively in sin, idolatry, and violent behavior. This is when the angels who fell with Satan (as opposed to those angels who took on human bodies and sinned, see Genesis 6:4) were assigned to set up a control center over the populated areas in ancient times.

Soon after Abel's death, another son named Seth was born to Adam and Eve, whose lineage remained pure to the time of Noah. Cain's lineage was different, though. Oddly, some of the very names given to Seth's descendants were the same names in Cain's family line. In Genesis 4:17-22, Moses listed Cain's lineage:

- Cain – Adam's son

- Enoch – Cain named a city after him

- Irad – son of Enoch

- Mehujael – son of Irad

- Lamech – engaged in polygamy, having two wives; he murdered two men

- Jabal – Lamech's son whose descendants lived in tents and raised cattle

- Jubal – Lamech's son who played a part in the development of music, as he was the father of those who play the harp and flute

- Tubal-cain – Lamech's son who learned to forge implements of bronze and iron.

Adam and Eve's sin was passed on through generations. Within humanity was a sin nature that could be fed by iniquity. As men and their sins multiplied, so did the influence of fallen angels. Cain committed the first murder over *religion*, just as today in the nations east of Eden, Islamic terrorists will claim their god is the greatest by shouting, "Allahu Akbar" as they are committing acts of violence and murdering innocent people. It is done in the name of religion. It is reminiscent of Cain's descendent Lamech, who committed a double homicide when he killed a man for wounding him and another young man for striking him (Gen. 4:23).

According to the Encyclopedia of Wars, out of 1,763 wars, 123 have been listed as religious in nature. These include the Crusader versus Muslim wars, the French versus Catholics and Huguenots, the Islamic conquests of the 7th and 8th centuries, and on up to the conflicts we witness today. Some are not outright wars but are national or civil uprisings that lead to violent conflicts over religious ideologies. For centuries, the Protestants and Catholics in England were in conflict over religious identity and persecution. The infighting between the

Sunni and Shi'ite Muslims has continued off and on since the seventh century AD. In India, conflict exists between Hindus and Muslims.

In the prophet Daniel's later years, the Persians, with substantial support from the Medes, captured Babylon in 539 BC. Babylonia was incorporated into the Persian (Achaemenid) Empire, which rose in the ancient land of Eden and beyond for about 220 years, until they were overthrown by the Grecian military general Alexander the Great in 330 BC.

In the time of Daniel, when the Persians took over Babylon, Daniel's prayers were hindered by a powerful demon spirit named "the prince of the kingdom of Persia" (Dan. 10:13). The Persian area has been a stronghold for powerful dark spirits for generations. The land east of Eden has also, for centuries, been the place of wars, fighting, and tribal clashes. It will be the center of the final prophetic conflicts as the rise of the ancient spirits unfolds.

CHAPTER 3

LAND OF THE ASSASSINS AND GATE OF THE GODS

The land of Persia and surrounding nations are connected to a dangerous warlike spirit. Most Arab nations can trace their early beginnings through either Esau, the son of Jacob, or through Abraham's son Ishmael, whose mother was Hagar. God Himself revealed the future of Ishmael when an angel appeared to a pregnant Hagar and advised her of the following:

- Your descendants will multiply so that there will be too many to count (Gen. 16:9).

- You will call your son Ishmael, because the LORD has heard your affliction (Gen. 16:11).

- He shall dwell in the presence of his brothers (Gen. 16:12). *Note: Isaac was a father of Israel.*

- He will be a wild man, and his hand shall be against every man, and every man's hand against him (Gen. 16:12).

The term *wild man* can have a secondary meaning and refer to a *wild donkey*. A wild donkey is independent, difficult to tame, and territorial enough to defend its space. The term *his hand against every man* can also allude to the tribal nature and in-house fighting that has occurred throughout history among some Arabs.

THE ASSASSINS

Between the 11th and 13th centuries AD, a powerful and dangerous group existed in the mountains of Syria and Persia called the Hashshashin, or the Assassins. They originated in Persia and were a religious sect of Shi'ite Muslims known as the Ismali from the Nizari lineage. They were headquartered in Persia, where Cain (the murderer) and his descendants settled before the great flood.

Some historical reports say that when the leaders of this group desired to kill a political or religious adversary, they would provide the assassin with the drug hashish, then promise that if he were to die while carrying out his assignment, the heavenly paradise would welcome him.

Multiple sources indicate that prior to Hamas terrorists attacking Israel on October 7, 2023, they took the drug captagon, which is called "the poor man's cocaine." It is a synthetic drug that is produced and abused throughout the Middle East and is said to have been used by ISIS. The drug would have lowered inhibitions and increased stamina which, along with a twisted and evil ideology, helps explain why these radicals performed horrific atrocities and laughed throughout the process.

Modern Iraq, a neighboring country to Iran, was part of Mesopotamia in ancient times. The pre- and post-flood history of this region is intriguing. After the flood, Noah's three sons—Shem, Ham, and Japheth—along with their children began to repopulate the earth. According to Jewish historian Josephus, the post-flood people made their homes in mountains, fearful that if they settled in valleys, another massive flood would reach them. It is also believed that when the waters receded after the flood, the corpses of those who drowned were found within the soil in the lower valleys.

This region became the headquarters of the world's first global form of government, led by a "mighty man" named Nimrod, who built the city of Babel (Gen. 11). Eventually, Nimrod began to rebuild cities in the land of Shinar, in what is today southern Iraq (Gen. 10:8-10). It was in this setting that Nimrod built or rebuilt nine cities, including his involvement with Babel.

In Babel, the people decided to build a tower that would reach into heaven (Gen. 11:4). It was believed the tower would also be used as a high place for stargazers and astrologers to ascend and interpret the positions of the stars and planets. Josephus wrote that Nimrod's true reason for such a high tower was to climb to the top and survive, should God choose once again to send a massive deluge to Earth.

Traditionally, the word "babel" is linked to the Hebrew word *balal*, which means "to confuse." In this case, it was the voices that would be confused. From Adam to Nimrod, the earth's inhabitants spoke one language. However, when Nimrod and the people tried to build a tower to reach heaven, God confused the languages of the people and scattered them in different directions, with each group being forced to join their specific language group (Gen. 11:1-9).

In the ancient Akkadian language, the name Babel is *Bab-ilani*, meaning "gate of the gods." This early meaning implies that the specific area where the tower of Babel was being built was considered a gate from which a specific god or gods had direct access as some type of spiritual portal.

The fact that early angelic and demonic prince activity was focused for hundreds of years among four major prophetic empires—the Assyrian, Babylonian, Medo-Persian, and Grecian Empires, is spiritually significant, considering that two of these four empires—the

Babylonian and Medo-Persian—were at least partially headquartered in ancient Babylonia. Assyria conquered Babylonia, and Alexander the Great planned to make the city of Babylon his capital, but he died before that plan was fulfilled.

BABEL AND THE WARFARE PORTAL

Why is this area so significant from a spiritual perspective? The answer could go back to the time prior to the creation of Eden. In ages past, before Adam was created, one-third of the angels participated in an attempted coup directed by Satan to overtake God's position, as he desired to exalt his throne above the stars of God and ascend the clouds to be like the Most High (Isaiah 14:12-14). Lucifer (Satan) was unsuccessful, as Jesus noted, "I saw Satan fall like lightning from heaven" (Luke 10:18). After being expelled from heaven, Satan set up a kingdom that gave him access to three realms:

1. *the air*, the atmosphere from the ground to the clouds. He is called "the prince of the power of the air" (Ephesians 2:2);

2. *the earth* as he "walks about seeking whom he may devourer" (1 Pet. 5:8);

3. *below the earth*, as he "walks up and down in the earth" (Job 1:7).

God's earthly gate (portal) is Jerusalem, which Jacob identified after experiencing a vision of angels on a ladder. He stated, "This is none other than the house of God, and this is the gate of heaven" (Gen. 28:17). This is why God directed Abraham to Salem (Jerusalem) to offer Isaac in the land of Moriah (Gen 22:1-14). The Mount of Moriah, which Abraham also called "The Mount of the Lord," is where Solomon's Temple would later be built in Jerusalem. In Solomon's time, God's cloud of glory descended with such brightness and weight at the Temple dedication that the priests fell to their faces, unable to stand (2 Chron. 5:14).

Just as Jerusalem is considered the gate of heaven, Babylon became the gate of bondage, captivity, idolatry, and world control. The Assyrian, Babylonian, Persian, and Greek leaders ruled from or had some control over Babylon for a total of 579 years. During that time, there were around forty-seven different kings or leaders who ruled from ancient Babylon at some point. This is why the stronger prince spirits and powerful angelic messengers were in continual conflict over the city and surrounding nations.

BABYLON: A POLITICAL AND SPIRITUAL HEADQUARTERS

The historic Old Testament city of Babylon is referred to in the books of Isaiah, Jeremiah, Daniel, and others. In Revelation, another city is identified as "Mystery Babylon." Thus, in Revelation there is an emphasis on Babylon's political, military, and religious impact. The ancient political Babylon is located in Iraq. The religious Babylon in Revelation is believed by some to be the city of Rome, Italy, which is the headquarters of the ancient Roman Empire. Rome is also the historic center for the Roman Catholic Church, with an estimated 1.4 billion baptized Catholics throughout the world.

After years of study, I believe that in ages past, when the fall of Satan occurred, he set up a kingdom with fallen angels in the same areas where civilization began. This area centered in ancient Mesopotamia, which became the site of Babel and the tower of Babel (Gen. 11) and later became Babylon and the Babylonian Empire (alluded to in Daniel).

For many years and thousands of hours, I have researched the scriptures to form an understanding of future prophetic events, including information about the future Antichrist. He will select one location, the area of ancient Babylon, as his early command center during the first forty-two months of the biblical tribulation. The second half of the tribulation, the final forty-two months, he sets his eyes on Jerusalem. First, he invades northern Africa, then marches to the Holy City and seizes the eastern half of Jerusalem for his military, political, and religious center, until Christ returns (Rev. 13; Zech. 14:4).

Satan's history began in an unknown time frame called ages past. He was expelled from the third heaven, the location of God's Throne and heavenly court (2 Cor. 12:1-4). He organized an army of rebellious angels that Jesus called "Satan's kingdom" (Luke 11:18). His prophetic future includes being cast out of his access to heaven's court and being permitted to empower the Antichrist for a season (Rev. 12:12).

At Christ's return, Satan will immediately be bound and confined under the earth in a place called the bottomless pit (Rev. 20:3). At the end of the thousand-year reign of Christ, he and the fallen angels will face their own heavenly judgment, and after his fate is sealed, he will spend eternity in the lake of fire (Rev. 20:10).

Until his obituary is sealed for eternity, Satan will initiate conflicts and persecution involving Israel, Jews, Christians, and the inhabitants of the whole world, in his battle for their eternal souls.

CHAPTER 4

SATAN'S ANGELIC PRINCE SPIRITS RULING THE NATIONS

Iran was ruled by monarchies from the 7th century BC until 1979 when the Shah, Mohammad Reza Pahlavi, was overthrown during the Islamic Revolution that was led by a Shi'ite cleric, Ayatollah Ruhollah Khomeini. Under the Shah, Iran was becoming modernized, and positive reforms were being implemented. Islamic religious leaders and their followers saw the reforms as morally corrupt and contrary to Islamic values. From the time of the Shah's overthrow until today, Iran has been tightly controlled by a Shi'ite regime under the rules of an Islamic Republic and strict sharia law. Once a monarchy, it is now a theocracy. The Ayatollah regime that has ruled Iran for years has controlled, oppressed, and killed an untold number of its own citizens, as well as citizens of other countries.

The dominating and authoritative prince spirit that has been operating behind the scenes and manipulating certain leaders is called the "prince of the kingdom of Persia" (Dan. 10:13, 20). In the days of Daniel, because of the intervention of the warring angel Michael, the prince of Persia was temporarily placed in check. This allowed the angel Gabriel to stand with and operate on God's behalf through the human kings, Darius of Media and Cyrus of Persia, under whom decrees were issued that permitted Jewish captives in Babylon to return and rebuild

Jerusalem and the sacred Temple. The Persian king also released the stolen Jewish Temple treasures back to the control of the Jews.

Gabriel remained with all the kings who ruled Persia for about 229 years. Gabriel informed Daniel that, following the Persian rule, the Greeks would form the next empire under the influence of a future "prince of Greece."

> *"Then he said, Do you know why I have come to you? And now I will return to fight with the [hostile] prince of Persia; and when I have gone, behold, the [hostile] prince of Greece will come."*
>
> – Daniel 10:20 (AMP)

For as long as human governments exist, countless angelic messengers will be on assignment to ensure that the ultimate and perfect will of God is not hindered, delayed, or interrupted by obscene prince spirits with opposing demonic strategies. God can and will interrupt or stop their activities.

Although there is no longer a Persian Empire with 127 provinces under their rule (Esther 1:1), the prince spirit that operated in the early centuries, the powerful prince of Persia, is still a dominating, invisible force over Iran and surrounding nations.

EXPOSING THE SEVEN HEADS OF THE DRAGON

In the book of Revelation, John used symbolism to describe the spiritual warfare instigated by Satan at the time of the end. Satan is called a *dragon* thirteen times in Revelation in the English translation. A dragon is a creature of mythology and legend, but its symbol is still found in several nations, including Japan, Vietnam, Korea, and China. The Chinese have used the symbol of a dragon since the Neolithic period, which their culture associates with things such as rain, prosperity, and the power and authority of their emperors. The Greek word for dragon in the King James translation of the Bible is a word that can allude to a serpent. Four times in the book of Revelation, Satan is referred to as a serpent (Revelation 12:9, 14, 15; 20:2).

Paul the apostle reminded readers of the serpent in Eden when he wrote, "The serpent beguiled [deceived] Eve..." (2 Cor. 11:3). Satan's sly and crafty methods are compared to a serpent, as a serpent can conceal itself before striking, adapt to its surroundings so as not to be detected, and eject deadly poison from its mouth.

Another symbol that has been interpreted to represent Satan is Leviathan, a name penned five times in the Old Testament. Leviathan is mentioned in Job 41:1-34 as a creature that is humanly impossible to defeat and is the king over the children of pride. Leviathan has heads (Psa. 74:14) and is also a sea creature (Psa. 104:26), a piercing and crooked serpent, and a dragon in the sea (Isa. 27:1).

Certain cultures have legends, often with roots developed in early civilization. Greek mythology has a many-headed serpent. Drawings discovered in excavations among the ruins in ancient Mesopotamia show a seven-headed serpent. The Hindus have a mythological multi-headed serpent that they consider divine and an upholder of cosmic law, as well as a mythological multi-headed serpent that churned the ocean to bring about immortality. In some cultures, the seven heads of the serpent represent evil and the influence of evil on the earth, which is the imagery of Satan in Revelation 12.

Four times throughout the book of Revelation, John described a dragon (Satan) or a beast with "seven heads" (Rev. 12:3; 13:1; 17:3, 7). The fallen angel Satan does not have seven heads growing out of his neck. This is symbolism describing the seven leading principality spirits that Satan has assigned to influence the empires that will negatively impact Israel, the Jews, and Jerusalem.

Many scholars believe that these seven heads refer to the seven primary empires that existed in the past and the seventh which will rise at the end of days:

1st head – the Egyptian Empire

2nd head – the Assyrian Empire

3rd head – the Babylonian Empire

4th head – the Persian (Media) Empire

5th head – the Grecian Empire

6th head – the Roman Empire

7th head – the East and West Union

Notice the conflicts arising in these empires. In *Egypt,* a destroying angel brought death to all their firstborn sons and animals, while the Hebrews were protected by lamb's blood placed on the outer door posts. Throughout the forty years that Israel wandered in the wilderness, the Almighty assigned a protective angel referred to as "the angel of God," who resided in a cloud by day and fire by night. This protective angel oversaw the entire nation of Israel (Exod. 14:19; 23:20).

When the *Assyrian* army entered Jerusalem with 185,000 armed troops, they covered the mountains around Jerusalem like a dark storm cloud. God assigned one angel of destruction to walk through the Assyrian military camps and unleash a sudden death plague that took out the entire army at once. By sunrise, 185,000 Assyrian troops were corpses (2 Kings 19:35, Isaiah 37:36).

With the *Babylonians,* God wrote with the finger of His hand on the banquet hall wall and warned Belshazzar, king of Babylon, that his kingdom would be divided and given to the Medes and Persians (see Dan. 5). That very night Belshazzar was slain, and Darius the Mede received the kingdom. Armies overtook Babylon while the Babylonian leaders were drunk on their wine.

Daniel 10 tells of a cosmic struggle between two of God's high-ranking messengers (Michael and Gabriel) and one of the heads of the serpent of Revelation, the prince of Persia. Because of the intervention of Michael and Gabriel, the *Persians* were friendly to Jews. However, after the time of Daniel, an enemy named Haman the Agagite was raised up among the Persians. Haman plotted to kill all Jews in 127 provinces. Esther, who was exiled to Persia as a Jewish orphan, won a beauty contest and became the wife of Ahasuerus, the Persian king. Her intercession and wisdom in exposing this evil plot spared the Jews from annihilation. This initiated a yearly Jewish celebration called Purim. Notice how the spirit of destruction against the Jews reappeared among the Persians and their leadership.

After the rise of the *Grecian Empire*, following Alexander the Great's sudden death, his generals divided the empire into several kingdoms. This gave rise to the spread of the Hellenistic culture and Greek influence. Eventually a Seleucid ruler arose named Antiochus IV Epiphanes, and he made a decree that his kingdom should follow practices of the Greek culture. Many Jews in Judea and Jerusalem resisted this, so Antiochus entered Jerusalem, tried to suppress Judaism, and demanded that the Jews follow his orders. He even offered a swine to his god on the altar of the Temple, thus defiling the sacred House of God. He outlawed the Jewish observance of the Sabbath, circumcision, and participation in yearly Jewish religious festivals. This led to the Maccabean Revolt, where God raised up a family known as the Maccabees who formed a militia to resist Antiochus and the Greeks.

Eventually the Maccabees defeated the Hellenistic king, restored control of Jerusalem back into the hands of the Jews, and rededicated the Temple in 164 BC. Scholars often compare the actions of Antiochus with the future Antichrist. Antiochus died in 164 BC in Persia. The book of Maccabees indicates that he fell out of his chariot during a military campaign and worms swarmed out of his body. He died not long afterward in a "most pitiable fate, among the mountains in a strange land" (2 Maccabees 9:5–28).

The *Roman Empire* followed the Grecian empire in the first century BC, taking control of land the Greek Empire had ruled. Rome used their soldiers to control the common people and keep peace. Any uprisings in Roman occupied areas were crushed by the merciless Roman troops.

The book of Acts records the spread of Christianity throughout Jerusalem, Judea, Samaria, and Asia Minor. It impacted multitudes, all the way to Rome, Italy, the center of the Roman Empire and the thrones of emperors. Powerful stories in the book of Acts reveal the involvement of angels assisting the righteous. Paul was harassed by a messenger (the Greek word is angel) of Satan—a hindering spirit assigned by Satan to continually bring opposition against Paul and his ministry. At times Paul had to flee towns, and in one instance he experienced a dangerous shipwreck (Acts 27). Paul was beaten three times, stoned once, chained in prison, and weakened through persecution and distress.

THE PRINCIPALITY WARNING

In his letter to the church of Ephesus, Paul revealed the true sources behind many intense spiritual, political, and personal struggles:

> *"For we do not wrestle against flesh and blood, but against principalities, against powers, against the rulers of the darkness of this age, against spiritual hosts of wickedness in the heavenly places."*
>
> – EPHESIANS 6:12 (NKJV)

These four—principalities, powers, rulers of darkness, and spiritual wickedness in the heavens—are all diabolical. They succeed when they have the body, hands, ears, or voice of a human vessel to operate through. Even Satan needed the body of a literal serpent to communicate with Eve.

Satan is called the tempter (Matt. 4:3). He confronted Christ face-to-face, when only he and Christ were in the wilderness setting. Every person can be tempted by acting on thoughts or by being influenced by other people's invitations or actions.

A principality is a spirit of the highest level of power and authority in the demonic kingdom. Some Greek scholars translate the phrase "wrestling against principalities" as "we wrestle against governments," as these spirits oversee and influence the highest levels of leadership in governments around the world. The greater the position, authority, or influence a person has achieved on earth, the higher the level of evil spirit assigned to them. Satan saves the highest spirits in his hierarchy for the people with the greatest influence and authority. A tyrant like Hitler did not simply operate under demonic influence; he was controlled like a puppet by one of the chief principalities.

There are seven major empires of biblical prophecy that lead to the eventual rise of the Antichrist. These prophetic empires existed with large populations long before the western hemisphere nations were organized. The nations and governments of the seven modern continents—Africa, Antarctica, Asia, Australia, Europe, North America, and South America—choose to either support or fail to support Israel and the Jewish people. In some manner, ancient prophetic empires were involved with supporting or fighting the Jews, Jerusalem, and the land known as Israel. The final Middle Eastern influencer organizes the "eighth kingdom" that rules for forty-two months (Rev. 17:11).

This eighth kingdom will be led by the Antichrist and ten nations, but the spirit behind him will be completely different from other prince spirits of past empires. Satan himself, not a high-ranking representative, will be in charge of events:

> *"Now the beast which I saw was like a leopard, his feet were like the feet of a bear, and his mouth like the mouth of a lion. The dragon gave him his power, his throne, and great authority."*
>
> – REVELATION 13:2 (NKJV)

This is an ideal example of something Satan told Christ, that he can deliver a kingdom to whomever he chooses (Luke 4:5-6). Certainly, it is not Satan, but God who raises up and removes kings and leaders (see Dan. 2:21). The only time Satan is in control of world governments is for forty-two months during the last half of the tribulation.

People have questioned why God would allow Satan to have control of world governments and their leaders for forty-two months (three-and-one-half years). Why permit the Antichrist and the False Prophet to have such unrestrained power?

First, there will no longer be a restrainer to control evil deeds. The true church is Satan's biggest roadblock on the earth today, and the gates of hell will not prevail against it (Matt. 16:18). The proclamation of God's Word lifts the veil of darkness and opens the minds and understanding of those in spiritual darkness (Eph. 1:18). The anointing of the Holy Spirit can bring wellness to a person's body, soul, and spirit when faith is infused with power from heaven. Believers have been given the power of agreement and authority over all the power of the enemy (Luke 10:19).

At the catching away and the resurrection of the dead in Christ, the population that remains will be spiritual apostates, lukewarm and backslidden former followers of Christ, pagans, worshippers of idols and false gods, and Jews who believed in God but not in Christ. It will be a planet full of people, some with evil intent, who will be forced to use any means necessary to survive the coming cataclysmic events.

Many of the tribulation coalitions will align for the purpose of survival. The ten kings give their kingdoms over to the Antichrist in one hour's time (Rev. 17:12-13). With the righteous being removed, and those with spiritual authority in the church no longer restraining evil through prayer, fasting, and action, Satan is given dominion and authority for forty-two months. Ecclesiastes 10:8 says, "He that digs a pit will fall into it; and whoever breaks a hedge, a serpent will bite him." When Job's hedge was removed, the enemy attacked him from every direction (Job 1:10-11). When the restraining power of the church is removed, the serpent, Satan, will be in control of the world's governments until the King of kings returns to rule (Rev. 20).

CHAPTER 5

A COSMIC WRESTLING MATCH

"And war broke out in heaven: Michael and his angels fought with the dragon; and the dragon and his angels fought, but they did not prevail, nor was a place found for them in heaven any longer. So the great dragon was cast out, that serpent of old, called the Devil and Satan, who deceives the whole world; he was cast to the earth, and his angels were cast out with him."

– REVELATION 12:7-9 (NKJV)

Michael is the only angel identified as an archangel in the sixty-six books of the Bible. The word archangel is mentioned twice, in Jude 9 where Michael contended with Satan over the body of Moses after he died, and in 1 Thessalonians 4:16, when at Christ's return all believers will hear "a shout, with the voice of the archangel, and with the trump of God." This archangel will be Michael, and he will be involved in the catching away of the saints and the resurrection of the dead in Christ. Immediately following this epic event, when the saints instantly arrive at the throne room of God in the third heaven, chaos will be released on the earth. Michael will become involved with tribulation events involving Jerusalem, Israel, and the Jewish people during the entire eighty-four months of the tribulation.

Michael's name is mentioned five times in scripture: Daniel 10:13, 21; 12:1; Jude 9; and Rev. 12:7). The Greek word archangel is *archagglos*, which is derived from two words; *archo,* referring to the first in power or authority, and *aggelos,* which means *messenger.* That can refer to a human messenger, including a pastor (Rev. 2 and 3), and a supernatural messenger, either an angel of God or an angel of Satan (2 Cor. 12:7).

Only two angels of God are named in the sixty-six books of the Bible: Michael the warring angel and Gabriel, God's messenger angel who brings messages from God to prophets and other people on earth. From a prophetic perspective, Michael deals primarily with Jerusalem, the Jewish tribes, and the nation of Israel. Gabriel and Michael are seen working together during the transitions of empires that are linked with prophecy. Gabriel was directly involved when the Medes and Persians overthrew the Babylonians (Dan. 10-11:1). Gabriel informed Daniel that he was sent from God to assist the kings of Persia and strengthen them, especially in their first year of rule, as this first year was when Darius permitted the Jews to return to Jerusalem and rebuild the house of God (Ezra chapter 1). These new rulers also allowed the Jews to cart their Temple treasures back to Jerusalem.

Gabriel remained with the kings of Persia in Babylon, and the behind-the-scenes spiritual conflict continued with this chief prince of Persia:

> *"Then he said, "Do you know why I have come to you? And now I must return to fight with the prince of Persia; and when I have gone forth, indeed the prince of Greece will come."*
>
> – Daniel 10:20 (NKJV)

In Daniel 8:16-27, Gabriel appeared to Daniel and revealed the future of Gentile empires. In Luke's gospel, Gabriel was sent from God to announce the birth of John the Baptist, and then to Mary in Nazareth to inform her that she would conceive and bring forth the Messiah (Luke 1:19, 26).

Michael's main objective is to be the "prince (protector) for Israel" (Daniel 10:21; 12:1). Gabriel assists the Gentile nations in participating and following through with their prophetic assignments. It is possible that Gabriel could be the unnamed angel that appears in warning dreams throughout the New Testament. Such examples are when an angel told Joseph to flee to Egypt, and when the wise men (who were Persians) were warned in a dream not to report the location of the infant Jesus to Herod. It is possible that Gabriel was the angel who appeared to Cornelius and connected him to Peter, which resulted in helping the Gentiles receive the New Covenant (Acts 10).

MICHAEL IS SATAN'S NIGHTMARE

In Revelation 12:7, John noted that both Satan and Michael each have angels that are under their authority. Satan deceived a third of the angels and convinced them to join him in rejecting God and organizing their own kingdom under Satan's leadership. John also wrote about Michael and his angels. If Satan has one third of the original angelic host, it is possible that Michael also has a third of the faithful who join with him in both cosmic wars and earthly assignments.

Michael's first conflict was reported in the book of Jude, where Michael contended with Satan over the body of Moses after he died. Satan would have desired that the Israelites discover Moses' body, mourn, build a monument to the great leader, then settle in Moab short of the Promised Land. After all, two and one-half tribes had already chosen to remain on the east side of the Jordan for their inheritance. By finding Moses' body, the other nine and one-half tribes could have been negatively influenced to follow their brothers. To prevent the rest of the tribes from delaying entry into the Promised Land, God Himself buried Moses in a location unknown to anyone. To this day, Moses' burial site remains a mystery (Deut. 34:6).

Since the death of Moses over 3,500 years ago, Michael the archangel has been personally assigned by the Lord to directly confront Satan when necessary. God prohibited Moses from entering the Promised Land because of one major act of disobedience. Israel wanted fresh water. Moses shouted at them saying, "Listen, you rebels! Must we fetch you water out of this rock?" The sin of Moses was not smiting the rock twice, as the rock was a symbol of Christ, and Christ indeed suffered twice; first through the Roman scourging, and then through Roman crucifixion. God rebuked Moses because he did not believe Him and did not uphold Him as holy in the eyes of the people (Num. 20:12). Moses did not express faith that God will give you water, but instead said, "Must we bring you water out of this rock?" (Num. 20:10).

Satan is an accuser of the righteous before God, day and night (Rev. 12:10). The accusations are for the purpose of disconnecting a person from God or attempting to bring up a sin that is already forgiven. After Moses was reprimanded by the Lord, he continued his ministry for many years; yet he fell short of entering the Promised Land based on God's decision in the wilderness.

Satan knew this, and we can assume he was contending (legally) against Michael, saying that he had a right to Moses' body because of his previous disobedience. Jude 9 tells us that Michael did not bring a railing accusation against Satan (the Greek word railing in Jude 9 means blasphemy or slander). This is because both Michael and Satan are high ranking angels, both were created by God in ages past, and both had angels under their command. Instead, Michael told Satan, "The Lord rebuke you," as Michael is representing God and not himself. Michael resisted Satan in the name of the highest authority in the universe, the Lord God Almighty, the God of Israel!

Michael's authority was also evident when Gabriel was given urgent prophetic secrets from God to deliver to Daniel. The prince of

Persia did not want these secrets made known to God's prophet Daniel. The strategy was to restrain Gabriel for an extended time, long enough for Daniel to become weak from fasting (Dan. 10:8) and eventually give up. Michael was given a direct order to intervene in this spiritual blockade and forcefully confront the evil prince who was creating the delay (Dan. 10). Under normal "atmospheric conditions," Gabriel would have arrived on the *first day* that Daniel consecrated himself to intercede (see Dan. 10:12). Notice a previous encounter with Gabriel:

> *"Now while I was speaking, praying, and confessing my sin and the sin of my people Israel, and presenting my supplication before the LORD my God for the holy mountain of my God, yes, while I was speaking in prayer, the man Gabriel, whom I had seen in the vision at the beginning, being caused to fly swiftly, reached me about the time of the evening offering."*
>
> – DANIEL 9:20-21 (NKJV)

Gabriel "flying swiftly" reveals the urgency he felt to enter Earth's atmosphere and explain the meaning of the strange symbolism Daniel was seeing in visions. Gabriel's presence was also detected by Daniel in chapter 8 after the ram and goat vision. He then saw someone standing before him who had the appearance of a man. He heard a voice between the banks of the Ulai River in Elam (southwestern Iran) commanding the man, whom Daniel identified as Gabriel, to make him (Daniel) understand this vision of the time of the end.

Throughout Daniel's seventy years in Babylon, Gabriel was his primary heavenly messenger. Michael, on the other hand, was overseeing the invisible warfare occurring over both Babylon and Persia, thus preventing any satanic prince angels from disrupting God purposes through the new leaders that rose throughout ancient, prophetic history.

WHEN MICHAEL STANDS UP

When the nation of Israel goes to war, Michael is called up for duty. To some extent, Israel's survival is in the authority of this mighty angel, as revealed by Daniel:

> *"At that time Michael, the great prince who protects your people, will arise. There will be a time of distress such as has not happened from the beginning of nations until then. But at that time your people–everyone whose name is found written in the book—will be delivered."*
>
> – Daniel 12:1 (NIV)

In Daniel 11:45 the angel reveals that the Antichrist will plant his headquarters in Jerusalem (between the seas; that is, the Dead Sea and Mediterranean). In Revelation chapters 11 to 13, the Antichrist is uniting his people (Muslims) in Jerusalem and killing the two Jewish prophets (Elijah and most believe Enoch). As these events unfold, this unleashes a cosmic clash between Michael and his angels and Satan's angelic, demonic entities in the upper atmosphere, as Satan and his angels are cast out from his heavenly stronghold to the earth (Rev. 12:7-12).

In Revelation 11:18, the raptured and resurrected believers will be judged (in Greek it is called the Bema judgement) and give an account of their life's activities, where they will either receive or lose rewards. In Revelation 12, Satan is a heavenly accuser (prosecutor) who presents alleged evidence against those in the assembly of the righteous. In the same chapter, Satan is cast down, while in chapter 13, the Antichrist and False Prophet take center stage in Jerusalem. When the Bema begins in the court of heaven, Satan and all his evil angels are expelled from heaven and will have no access at the heavenly judgment to bring charges or allegations against God's servants, prophets, saints, and those who fear His name. As Paul wrote, "Who shall bring a charge against God's elect? It is God that justifies" (Rom. 8:33 NKJV).

Michael and his angels will be continually active in the last days to oversee activities transpiring in Israel, including wars against Israel and the Jewish people. Paul wrote that, "All Israel shall be saved" (Rom. 11:26). A remnant shall be saved out of the tribulation (Rev. 14:1-3); a second remnant will be saved by escaping into the wilderness during the tribulation (Rev. 11); and some survivors of the tribulation who neither worshipped the Antichrist nor accepted his mark will accept Christ when He returns to earth and they see the wounds in His hands (see Zech. 13:6).

Even though a third of the angels followed Satan, two-thirds remained loyal. This means that for one evil angel against us, God has two that are for us. Also remember that, in every biblical example, Michael always successfully defeated Satan and his agenda. Third, believers have been given authority over all the power of the enemy (Luke 10:19). Elisha saw a mountain full of angelic host and said to his servant, "Do not fear, for those who are with us are more than those who are with them" (2 Kings 6:16-17). It also explains Paul's admonition in Romans 8:31, "If God is for us, who can be against us?"

The cosmic confrontation between Michael and his angels and Satan and his angels will purge the heavenly realm of demonic and fallen angel influence, as the old serpent and his angels are cast to the earth. In Revelation 12, the heavens will rejoice at this event. However, the world will be targeted for a time of great tribulation, "such as never was since there was a nation" (Dan. 12:1). The wrath of the Lamb (Rev. 6:16), the wrath of God (Rev. 16:1), the rage of the nations (Rev. 11:18), and the wrath of Satan will all collide. Global destruction will unfold, beginning with the opening of the seven sealed scrolls and followed by the trumpet and bowl judgments, and shake the cities, the nations, the heavens, and the earth.

Michael the archangel has been Israel's guardian since the birth of the nation, and he is God's strongest warring prince angel. He is actively involved in all these end-time events involving Israel, Jerusalem, and the Jewish people.

CHAPTER 6

WHY DO MANY MUSLIMS DISLIKE THE JEWS AND ISRAEL?

If you ask someone today why so many Muslims either resent or hate Jews, a common answer will be, "Because the Jews are occupying Islamic lands in Palestine." However, this politically charged answer is not the root of the problem. To uncover the root of this animosity, it is important to grasp the historical background of Islam, including the death of Islam's founder Mohammad.

The Romans were occupying the Holy Land when they destroyed Jerusalem in AD 70. In the year 135, following the third Jewish uprising known as the Bar Kokhba Revolt, the Romans deliberately renamed the land that had been known as Judea and Samaria, calling it "Syria Palaestina." The Romans did this primarily to punish the Jews and erase their identity from the land.

Hundreds of years later, when Muhammad lived in Arabia, the Byzantine Christians were living in the Holy Land. The Byzantine Period lasted from around AD 333 to 633, during which time the Byzantines constructed beautiful and elaborate churches on the sacred biblical sites.

Meanwhile, in Arabia, there were numerous Arabs, Jews, and Christians scattered throughout, with two of the most noted cities being Mecca and Medina. In Mecca, there was a well of fresh water for caravans. In Medina resided many Jewish tribes who had likely fled the Holy Land during Roman rule.

Most Arabs in Arabia at that time were polytheists—that is, they worshipped a pantheon of different gods, most of which were associated with heavenly bodies that were assigned various attributes and had alleged power over earthly events. They worshipped and practiced rituals at shrines and temples, including the cubical shrine in Mecca called the Kaaba, a pagan worship center where many of their gods were housed.

Various Christian clans also lived in Arabia when Mohammad went to the mountains and claimed that an angel, whom he believed to be Gabriel, gave him revelations. Muhammad said that this angel continued to give him revelations from God (Allah) over the next two decades. Muhammad was illiterate, but he recited what he heard, and his followers wrote it down.

Around the year 613, Muhammad began to preach his revelations, and some considered him a prophet because of the angelic visitations. In the beginning, Mohammad called Jews and Christians "people of the book." At first they listened to his messages, but later they rejected and mocked him for various reasons, and they often engaged him in religious arguments. As he faced increased persecution, he and his followers moved to Medina where Muhammad became a political and spiritual leader.

He tried to convert people to his belief system diplomatically and peacefully, but when that didn't work, he used military action. Followers of Islam began to raid villages, capture people, and take spoil. Coinciding with the violence, Muhammad's religious views changed, and he considered those who refused to accept him and his prophecies as infidels who deserved death. While many were killed, some converted and others chose to pay a tax (jizya) to live as a non-Muslim under Muslim rule. The revelation about killing infidels (non-Muslims) was allegedly given to Muhammed after he arrived in Medina and after he faced mockery and persecution.

Muhammad led twenty-seven battles, while ordering his military to conduct another sixty or so. Early sources connected to Muhammad suggested that six hundred to nine hundred Jewish men were killed during raids in Medina, while women and children were enslaved. Muhammad claimed to be doing this based on Jewish law.

THE POISONING OF MOHAMMAD

A story of Mohammad's strange and perhaps untimely death has been passed down for centuries. The Islamic Hadith, a book filled with commentary of early Muslims who followed Mohammad, observed his life and teachings, and recorded everything after his death, recalls a story of Muhammad being served poisoned meat. As the story goes, a Jewish woman whose father, husband, and brother had been killed in a battle with Muhammad's army sought revenge for their deaths by roasting a lamb (a few commentators later said a goat) and poisoning a portion of it. When Mohammad started chewing it, he knew something was wrong and spat it out. One of his companions ate the lamb and died. The story says that when Mohammad realized what had happened, he asked the Jewish woman why she would do such a thing. Her reply was that she was testing him to see if he really was a prophet. If so, he would know the meat was poisoned. If not, he would eat it and they would be rid of him. Sources differ on whether the Jewish woman was killed or forgiven and allowed to live.

It is reported that Muhammad used to tell his wife Aisha that he "still feels the pain caused by the food I ate at Khaybar, and at this time, I feel as if my aorta is being cut from that poison."

Even though the primary Islamic view is that Muhammad died from an illness, there were Islamic scholars who speculated that he died from a politically motivated poisoning. The story that Muhammad was poisoned is still noted and passed on by some Muslims today.

Throughout his life, Mohammad had eleven wives. He had only one wife for a while, and he was married to her for twenty-five years. His other ten marriages occurred after she died. Five were widows and at least two were Jewish captives. His youngest wife was Aisha, with whom he had a marriage contract when she was six years old, while the marriage was consummated when she was nine. Muhammad issued a special provision for himself to marry this many wives, while other Muslim men were limited to four wives.

Mohammad lived for approximately five years after the attempted poisoning, and it is said that he suffered much before dying in the year 632 at almost sixty-three years of age. Even though he lived well beyond the attempted poisoning and it could not have been the cause of his death, many Muslims still think a Jew was responsible for killing him. This gave a reason for a seed of Muslim hatred to be planted against Jews.

INFIDELS OCCUPYING ISLAMIC LANDS

Most Arabs who live in the Holy Land today refer to themselves as Palestinians. Some lived or had family living in the land before Israel was rebirthed as a nation in 1948, since most records indicate that two-thirds of the people living there in 1948 were Christian or Muslim Arabs. One-third of the people who lived there were Jews. Many Arabs who live in the Holy Land today have ancestral roots in surrounding countries such as Egypt, Syria, and Jordan.

There are two primary religions practiced among the Arabs who live in Israel: Muslim and Christian. While the majority are Muslim,

Why Do Many Muslims Dislike the Jews and Israel?

many can be considered non-practicing and call themselves Muslim by birth and in name only. Some are Christian, predominately Catholic, Orthodox, and some Coptic.

Many groups and empires have ruled the land of Israel throughout its history. The Bible tells us about the monarchy that ruled after the Hebrew people left Egypt and returned to the Land of Canaan. Saul, David, and Solomon served as kings under the United Monarchy from approximately 1030 BC to 928 BC. After Solomon's death, the kingdom was divided between the Northern Kingdom, which was eventually conquered by Assyria, and the Southern Kingdom of Judah, which was conquered by the Babylonians around 136 years later.

Then came other conquerors—the Persians, Greeks, Romans, Byzantines, Arabs, Crusaders, Mamelukes, Ottomans, and the British. It was under the British Mandate that Israel was given a state, which was carved from the biblical land that the pagan Romans had renamed Syria Palaestina.

There wasn't much to see in the land of Israel when Mark Twain visited there in the 19th century. He wrote in *The Innocents Abroad* that the land was dismal, desolate, void of inhabitants, wholly given over to weeds—a silent mournful expanse. There was hardly a tree or a shrub anywhere, and even the olive tree and cactus had almost deserted the country.

Prior to 1948, Jewish people were scattered throughout the world, even in nations that are now considered predominately Muslim. Many lived in Arab nations, including Egypt, Libya, Morocco, Tunisia, Iraq, Syria, Algeria, and Yemen. In those days, before the formal establishment of Israel as a state, some of these countries were politically more moderate than they are today, and some even had a significant Christian population.

Figures vary depending on the source, but Jewish Business News reports that the world's Jewish population on the eve of World War II was 16.6 million. In 1948, on the eve of the establishment of the state of Israel, the world's Jewish population was 11.5 million. On the eve of World War II, 449,000 Jews lived in Israel. On the eve of the establishment of the state of Israel, 650,000 Jews lived in Israel.

Relationships between Arabs and Jews who lived in the land before 1948 were marked by periods of peace between episodes of violence and conflict, primarily because of the upheaval and transition happening throughout the Middle East. The rise of Zionism, which is defined as the belief that Jews have a right to self-determination and should have their own state in their ancestral homeland, led to further conflict with the Arabs. In 1929, religious tensions surrounding the Western Wall led to violence and a significant number of Jewish casualties throughout the land.

On November 29, 1947, the United Nations announced a partition to officially establish a Jewish state. Immediately an Arab leader announced that the Arabs would drench the soil with their last drop of blood and fight for every inch of their country. A protest strike was announced, and riots broke out. In a few short months, thousands of Jews, Arabs, and British had been killed in the riots. The United Nations blamed the Arabs for the violence, and Jamal Husseini, the Arab leader who had encouraged the fighting months earlier, took full responsibility.

The state of Israel was formally established on May 14, 1948. The very next day, war broke out. The armies of Egypt, Transjordan, Syria, Lebanon, and Iraq joined together to fight the Jews in the newly established state of Israel. Azzam Pasha, Secretary-General of the Arab League, declared that this would be a war of extermination, a momentous massacre that would be remembered like the Crusades.

The Jewish people were at a distinct disadvantage because they had a small military and no weapons that could fight off established armies from five surrounding Arab countries. The Israeli army had

18,900 mobilized fighters, nine obsolete planes, and no tanks. Over six thousand Israelis were killed in the war. Agricultural fields and citrus groves that had taken Jewish farmers decades to build were destroyed. The War of 1948, also known to Israel as the War of Independence, began on May 15, 1948 and ended on July 20, 1949. About one percent of both the Jewish and Arab populations in Israel were killed during this war. Over time, the Arab countries signed armistice agreements with Israel.

The situation never fully settled down, as Arab leaders continued to express their desire to completely eradicate Israel. A war started by Egypt, Syria, and Jordan in 1967 is known as the Six-Day War. Israel drove Jordanian forces out of the eastern half of the city of Jerusalem and most of the area referred to as the West Bank. Israel captured the Old City of Jerusalem, the Golan Heights from Syrian forces, and the Gaza Strip and the Sinai Peninsula from Egypt. Arab forces suffered severe casualties, while documentaries have been produced that show the supernatural events that allowed Israel to miraculously win the war, despite their significant military disadvantages.

With the looming threat of wars, many Arabs crossed over into Jordan, some went to Syria, and others to Lebanon out of fear. Some were placed in refugee camps within these countries. Many remain there to this day, even though the people are free to leave. Some have chosen to resettle in other countries. Further discussion of wars, refugee status, and ongoing Israeli-Arab conflict is beyond the scope of this book, but this gives the reader a general idea of the history behind the conflict in the Middle East.

The formation of a Palestinian State within Israel has been discussed for decades. From the perspective of some Arabs, the Israelis are occupying their land. From a biblical and Jewish perspective, this has been the Jewish homeland since the time of Abraham, Isaac, and Jacob. Even though they were taken captive at times by people and empires who conquered their land, God always brought them back.

Islam was organized in the seventh century AD. This was over five hundred years after the destruction of the Second Temple by the Romans in the year 70, and over eleven hundred years after King Cyrus of Persia permitted the captive Jews to return to the land in 538 BC to rebuild the house of God (see Ezra 1:1-4).

Going back to 1030 BC takes us to the beginning of the United Kingdom, the Israelite monarchial period under kings Saul, David, and Solomon. David purchased Mount Moriah from a Jebusite, so that the mountain could be the site of God's Temple that was later built by his son Solomon. Go back in time another eight hundred years and history takes us to the time when Abraham presented his son Isaac on Mount Moriah and offered tithe to Melchizedek, the first king and priest of God (Gen. 22 and Gen. 14).

Abraham was called a Hebrew (Gen. 14:13) and his early descendants were known as Hebrews. Several passages in Exodus refer to God as "the God of the Hebrews." After the death of Solomon, when the kingdom of Israel was divided, the people from Judea identified themselves as Jews, which is the name that the Jewish people call themselves today.

Here is the challenge Israel faces. Historically illiterate people (especially in Western nations) and Middle Eastern religious bias have caused many people to insert their personal opinions into the narrative because they don't believe anything written in the Bible. These groups often falsely charge that Christians and Jews changed the Torah stories to confirm their own personal theology to benefit Israel and the Jews.

With the writings in the Islamic Quran and the negative comments made about Jews (and Christians); with some Muslims believing the death of Mohammad was caused by a Jewish woman poisoning him; and with certain Arabs believing that Israel is occupying the land and has no rights to "Palestine," it helps explain why there are so many seeds of hatred producing the fruit of violence throughout the Middle East and parts of the world. The Antichrist will use this hatred to build his army, inspire his ten kings, and eventually attack Jerusalem while making one final attempt to destroy Israel and the Jews.

What is the true purpose behind the satanic goal of annihilating Israel, Jerusalem, and the Jews? In my opinion, the answer is not that complicated. There are two dichotomous kingdoms with clashing ideologies and goals: the kingdom of God and the kingdom of Satan. The satanic kingdom operates by killing, stealing, and destroying (John 10:10). Satan, our adversary, is a liar and the father of lies (John 8:44).

God, however, is not a man, that He should lie (Num. 23:19). Paul also noted:

> "Thus God, determining to show more abundantly to the heirs of promise the immutability of His counsel, confirmed it by an oath, that by two immutable things, in which it is impossible for God to lie, we might have strong consolation, who have fled for refuge to lay hold of the hope set before us."
>
> – HEBREWS 6:17-18

When God marked a covenant agreement with Abraham, the Almighty could not make an oath any higher than Himself, as He is the Most High God. Thus, God "swore by Himself" the oath (Heb. 6:13), meaning that He would not and could not lie to Abraham, but would bring the promises to pass.

Since God cannot lie and since He is absolute light and truth, what if the adversary could find one time when God lies to someone? That one lie would void every promise God made and place Him on the level of a deceiver. God made covenants, and covenant is the key. God's covenants include binding promises that He made to Abraham, David, and others.

Satan's goal is to see God's covenants nullified. If the adversary could completely wipe out Jerusalem, Israel, and the Jews, he would:

- void God's covenant with David, that he and his lineage would rule over Israel forever and the kingdom will be everlasting (2 Samuel 7:8-11);
- nullify the covenant God made with Abraham to make him a great nation (Gen. 12:2) and for his countless descendants to inherit the land (Gen. 13:14-17);
- cause God's covenant promises to become lies.

Throughout the ages, there have been nations, armies, and prince spirits of darkness that have conspired against God and His promises. They have attempted to overtake Jerusalem and Israel, and remove the Jewish people from their land and scatter them around the world. However, all of man's demonically inspired evil strategies have failed. Israel still exists, Jerusalem is the capital, and the Jews have returned from the nations.

Let God be true and every man a liar! The enemy cannot destroy what God has spoken, for His word shall not pass away (Matt. 24:35). Psalm 89:4 says it all: "My covenant I will not break, nor alter the word that has gone out of my lips." Satan will never destroy the covenants of God, because God cannot lie.

CHAPTER 7

PROPHETIC VISIONS OF THE SERPENT OF GAZA

Since the mid-1980s, I have visited Israel almost forty times, along with those joining our tour groups. I have made pilgrimages in times of peace and during seasons of conflict, yet not once did I feel threatened, fearful, or intimidated. I have seen firsthand how rock throwing and tire burning protests were staged for the benefit of international media. The signs were prepared in advance and written in English so they could be read by the American audience, in hopes of shifting and reshaping Americans' opinions of Israel. Enemies inside Israel leading the charge have included various terrorist groups and their supporters, including Hamas, whose main objective is the destruction of Israel and the Jews.

Hamas emerged as a branch of the Muslim Brotherhood in 1988 after the first Palestinian intifada. Hamas has a political and a military wing. The political wing is involved in propaganda and negotiations, while the military wing has created conflict with Israel by engaging in protests, killing Israelis through suicide bombings, and shooting an untold number of missiles into Israel for years. This culminated with the vicious and demonic attacks on October 7, 2023. These terrorists have been like serpents, hiding until it was time to strike unexpectedly.

Take a look at the history of the southwest coastal region of the land of Canaan, part of which is known today as the Gaza Strip. In early biblical times, the Canaanites lived there. From the time of the Judges into the time of King David, a group of sea people known as the Philistines ran off the Canaanites and settled the land. The Bible says the Philistines came from the coastland of Caphtor, which most scholars believe to be the island of Crete.

The Philistines controlled five cities, known as the Pentapolis: Ashdod, Ashkelon, Ekron, Gath, and Gaza. Goliath was a Philistine giant that the Bible refers to as Goliath from Gath. The area the Philistines controlled was named Philistia. Most Bible translations use Philistia, while the King James Version in Joel 3:4 uses Palestine.

As mentioned previously, after the destruction of the Temple in AD 70 and after the Bar Kokhba Revolt in AD 135, the Romans changed the name of the land of Judea and Samaria to Syria Palaestina. It had gone from being called the land of Canaan, the Promised Land, or the land of the Hebrews (Genesis 40:15) to the Southern Kingdom of Judea and the Northern Kingdom (Samaria) after the death of King Solomon. Then it was renamed Palaestina by the Romans, and that name remained until 1948 when the land was renamed Israel. Around 135 BC, the Roman emperor Hadrian also renamed Jerusalem to honor his family and a Roman god, calling it Aelia Capitolina.

The first biblical mention of the land of Israel is found in 1 Samuel 13:19. This identified the lineage of promise from Abraham to Isaac to Jacob, whose name God changed to Israel (Gen. 32:28). The earliest non-biblical mention of Israel is found inscribed on the Merneptah Stele that originated in Egypt in 1208 BC. Similar discoveries were made around three to four hundred years later in Jordan, Tel Dan, Turkey, and Iraq.

ANCIENT GAZA PROPHECIES

The Gaza region has long been a headquarters for Israel's enemies. Mentioned nineteen times in the Bible, Gaza is where Samson met Delilah, who uncovered the secret of his covenant (Judg. 16:21). The Philistines gouged out Samson's eyes so that he could not see his enemies. In similar modern fashion, Hamas terrorists would hide themselves in underground tunnels to prevent Israeli intelligence from seeing them.

Several biblical prophets allude to Gaza's destruction. The book of Amos mentions God punishing Damascus, then speaks about a fire on the wall of Gaza that will devour the palaces. In modern terms the wall can allude to a border area that is breached (Amos 1:7).

Isaiah gives an important prediction concerning the area of Palestina (specifically, the southwest area of Israel known today as the Gaza Strip):

> "Rejoice not thou, whole Palestina, because the rod of him that smote thee is broken: for out of the serpent's root shall come forth a cockatrice, and his fruit shall be a fiery flying serpent. And the firstborn of the poor shall feed, and the needy shall lie down in safety: and I will kill thy root with famine, and he shall slay thy remnant. Howl, O gate; cry, O city; thou, whole Palestina, art dissolved: for there shall come from the north a smoke, and none shall be alone in his appointed times. What shall one then answer the messengers of the nation? That the LORD hath founded Zion, and the poor of his people shall trust in it."
>
> – Isaiah 14:29-32 (KJV)

Zephaniah 2:4 reads, "For Gaza shall be forsaken, and Ashkelon a desolation...." The same prophet wrote in Zechariah 9:5, "Gaza also shall see it, and be very sorrowful...and the king shall perish from Gaza...."

Isaiah spoke of the "serpent's root." From Genesis 3 to Revelation 20, the Bible symbolizes Satan as a serpent. The cockatrice mentioned by Isaiah is a dangerous hissing viper, so dangerous that if a person is bitten, it normally causes death within minutes. In the natural world, a fiery *flying* serpent does not exist. However, when Israelites were bitten by serpents in the desert, bringing death to those bitten, the serpents were called, "fiery serpents" (Num. 21:6). Theologians believe the "fiery" term can refer to the color of the serpent. The word "fiery" comes from the Hebrew word saraph, which is the same word used to describe the seraphim, the angels that minister before God's throne. It can also allude to a burnt bronze color. To bring healing to the Israelites, Moses built a "fiery serpent," which was actually a bronze pole with a bronze serpent, intended to be symbolic of Christ on the pole taking the sins of the world (John 3:14-15).

Israel's most important cities, such as Jerusalem and Tel Aviv, are located north and northeast of Gaza. In modern understanding, we have seen smoke coming from the north in the recent military attacks that followed the October 7 Hamas attacks on Israel. We have all watched the smoke rising from buildings as they are hit throughout the Gaza.

THE FOUR HORSEMEN

In the Bible, numbers and colors are significant and hold spiritual meaning. In the book of Revelation, at the beginning of the Great Tribulation, John saw four horses of different colors, each with a particular rider who conquers and brings war, violence, famine, food rationing, and death to much of the world. The horses and their colors are:

- the white horse (Rev. 6:2) - rides throughout the earth to conquer nations;

- the red horse (Rev. 6:4) - takes peace from the earth so that men slay each other;

- the black horse (Rev. 6:5) - induces famine, food shortages, and exorbitant food prices;

- the pale (literally green) horse (Rev. 6:8) - brings war, famine, pestilence, and death to over one-fourth of the world

All four of these colors—white, red, black, and green—are symbolically connected to leaders, cultures, and flags throughout Islamic history. Green is strongly associated with Islam, perhaps because Muhammad's banner and cloak were said to be green. The Shi'ite Fatimid Caliphate in North Africa used green. Notice that the arm and headbands worn by Islamic militias are often green.

White was said to be worn by Muhammad during some rituals and battles. The Umayyad Dynasty (661 - 750 AD), who ruled from their capital of Damascus, used white banners, with white also being their symbol of mourning. The color is associated with resistance and martyrdom in some Shi'ite circles.

Red is said to represent blood, sacrifice, courage, and a struggle for freedom. It was connected to the Islamic rulers of Andalusia (AD 756 - 1031), who dominated Libya, Tunisia, Morocco, and Algeria (Northern Africa) at one time. The Kharijites, Hashemites, and North African Islamic dynasties have used red in some manner.

Black symbolizes religious revolution, revenge, and authority. In Shi'ite Islam, it is also linked to mourning. Note that women in many Islamic countries and cultures are forced to wear black garments from head to foot. The Abbasid Caliphate (762–1258 CE), who overthrew the Umayyads and ruled from Baghdad, used black.

In much of the Islamic world, one or more of these colors is featured on the countries' national flags. Decades ago, I noticed something interesting about the Palestinian flag. The same four colors given the four apocalyptic horsemen in the book of Revelation are the same colors of the Palestinian flag—white, black, green, and red.

The four colors were originally combined on a flag that was created to represent the Arab Revolt against the Ottomans in 1916. The Palestinian Liberation Organization officially adopted the flag in 1964, and the flag is still used today to represent "liberation through armed struggle." The four Arab dynasties represented on the flag are:

1. white – the Umayyads (661–750 AD)

2. black – the Abbasids (750–1517 AD)

3. green – the Fatimids (909–1171 AD)

4. red – the Hashemites (1916-present).

Islamic mosques are found throughout Israel. The minaret, the tall cylinder-shaped tower where a man calls Muslims to prayer five times a day, is supposed to be the highest structure in any village, town or city. It is intended to be seen and heard by everybody. The crescent moon atop a mosque was adopted from other cultures, especially during the Seljuk Dynasty, and the crescent moon and star became a symbol for Islam under Ottoman rule. Green florescent lights that remain lit at the mosque throughout the night make it visible from a long distance.

THE PALESTINIAN LINK

The Isaiah prophecy reveals that from Palestina will come a "flying fiery serpent." Israel often used the lion as their emblem, as the tribal symbol of the tribe of Judah is a lion (Gen. 49:9). The territory of the tribe of Judah included Bethlehem and part of Jerusalem, who shared the Jerusalem border with the tribe of Benjamin. When the war with Iran broke out, Prime Minister Benjamin Netanyahu noted a scripture in the book of Numbers, speaking of Israel, where Balaam the seer said:

> "God brought him forth out of Egypt; He hath as it were the strength of an unicorn: He shall eat up the nations his enemies, And shall break their bones, And pierce them through with his arrows. He couched, he lay down as a lion, And as a great lion: who shall stir him up? Blessed is he that blesseth thee, and cursed is he that curseth thee."
>
> – Numbers 24:8-9 (KJV)

The military campaign against Iran was called "The Rising Lion," indicating that Israel had been crouching as a lion. However, the attacks from Iran, called the head of the serpent, had stirred the spirit of a lion in the hearts of the political and military leaders of Israel. Note this verse in Isaiah:

> "The burden of the beasts of the south: Into the land of trouble and anguish, From whence come the young and old lion, The viper and fiery flying serpent, They will carry their riches upon the shoulders of young asses, And their treasures upon the bunches of camels, To a people that shall not profit them."
>
> – Isaiah 30:6 (KJV)

A symbol of ancient Israel is the lion. The lion has also been an emblem of England since the twelfth century. America's roots are British, meaning that symbolically, we are a young lion. The old lions (ancient empires) and the young lion (America) have assisted Israel in their recent wars. The victories Israel is now experiencing could bring about a season of peace. However, eventually the beast (remember that the Antichrist kingdom is the "beast kingdom" in Daniel and Revelation), will arise from the south to take spoil and riches. Gaza is in the southwestern part of Israel, and Egypt is to the south. Prophetic verses in Daniel explain how the Antichrist will overthrow the horn of Africa, including Egypt, to gain the treasure:

> "He shall also enter the Glorious Land, and many countries shall be overthrown; but these shall escape from his hand: Edom, Moab, and the prominent people of Ammon. He shall stretch out his hand against the countries, and the land of Egypt shall not escape. He shall have power over the treasures of gold and silver, and over all the precious things of Egypt; also the Libyans and Ethiopians shall follow at his heels."
>
> – Daniel 11:41-43 (NKJV)

Many of the religious, political, and governmental leaders in Islamic nations view the Israeli military as aggressors and enemies of Islam. While some in the Gulf states and more modern Islamic nations are glad to see the defeat of radical Islamic terrorism, this breaking of the serpent's teeth will only initiate temporary peace and security. Eventually, the serpent (Satan) will raise up one man, whom Satan will give a throne for a time (one year) times (two years) and dividing of time (6 months), or three and one-half years (Dan 7:25, Rev. 13:5).

The fallen angel, Satan, who will be unleased on the earth for a season of terrible destruction and deep deception, is described by John as a "great red dragon" (Rev. 12:3). The Greek word *red* in that verse is *pyrros*, which denotes a fiery red color that evokes the look of flame, blood, and burning heat. John called Satan a dragon. This word in Greek is *drakon*, referring to a serpent, which has always been a symbol for Satan.

It appears that Hamas in Gaza has experienced a massive setback due to the Israeli war that followed the October 7 massacre and kidnapping of over a thousand Israeli citizens by Hamas terrorists. Thousands of terrorists are dead, including many military commanders and high-level leaders. Many buildings in the Gaza Strip have been either destroyed or damaged.

A fiery serpent will emerge because of the war in Gaza. This prophecy is parallel to the vision of John, who saw a great red dragon (serpent), identified as Satan, overseeing the wars and persecution in the future. He will leverage the unity of the ten nation's kings and the Antichrist himself.

In 2024 and 2025, so far Israel has fought or been involved in terrorist conflicts on six different fronts: Gaza, the West Bank, Lebanon, Syria, Iran, and Yemen. These territories are under Islamic control and show that radicals have been supplied the money and weapons to operate. Much of the assistance came through the Shi'ite leaders of Iran.

Based on my knowledge of the Bible, Israel and her allies will temporarily set back these military terrorist movements for an unknown season. Making peace will become the main objective, at least for a time. Eventually, the "deadly wounds" will be healed and the final kingdom (which I believe will be Islamic) will arise as a beast with "iron teeth" that will devour and break into pieces its enemies (Dan. 7:7). Organizing such a powerful new empire will require a headstrong and controlling personality under the influence of the strongest spirits in the dark kingdom.

The early church taught that there are seven chief angels that are considered the highest ranking in the heavenly army of God. In Revelation 12:3, Satan has seven heads, which are seven prince spirits that answer directly to him. Just as there are angels over nations, there are prince spirits over empires.

The strongest spirits are those that have overseen and influenced the leaders of the empires of history and Bible prophecy. The king, dictator, or president may die and be placed in a tomb, but the ruling spirit can remain in the same city or nation and still do its work. Christ also taught that one spirit can find seven others to join ranks and return to a person. This is why some nations are defeated in war, yet they reorganize and return again with new leaders and a new army of death.

CHAPTER 8

WHEN THE ABYSS RELEASES THE DESTROYERS

The Earth is a remarkable, dynamic planet that God created to produce and sustain life. Basic geology tells us that the Earth's layers are the crust, the mantle, and the core.

The crust is the thin outer layer that supports life, the layer where cities and nations are built, and where rivers, streams, and oceans flow. The continental crust ranges from about eighteen to forty-three miles thick.

The Mohorovičić discontinuity (Moho) is a boundary between the Earth's crust and mantle. It separates the crust from the upper mantle.

The mantle, containing denser rocks, minerals, and water, is an astonishing 1,802 miles thick and makes up most of Earth's volume. The mantle helps regulate thermal balance to stabilize the overall temperature, which is a remarkable feat, considering that the coolest temperature close to the crust is around 1,000 degrees Fahrenheit. Activity within the mantle contributes to volcanoes, earthquakes, and mountain formation. Seismologists say there are mountain-like structures at the base of the mantle that are estimated to be three to five times higher than Mount Everest.

The core, composed mostly of iron and nickel, is over three thousand miles beneath the surface of the Earth. Scientists estimate that the outer core could be as hot as 10,800 degrees Fahrenheit and the inner core as hot as the sun, at 12,000 degrees Fahrenheit. NASA recently published an article stating that the core is slowing reversing rotation, which could affect the Earth's magnetic field behavior and slightly alter the length of days.

Keep in mind that no scientist or seismologist has ever conducted a research trip to the mantle and core of the Earth, so their information is based on knowledge gained through seismology (earthquakes, scans of the earth), gravity measurements, physics lab experiments, magnetic field studies, computer models, and so on.

THE MYSTERIOUS ABYSS

Revelation 9:1 speaks of the "bottomless pit," a place mentioned seven times in Revelation. The Greek word is *abyssos,* or in English, *abyss.* It describes a deep place without a bottom, referring to a sizeable area under the crust of the Earth that seems to have no end.

In ancient times, the word was used to describe the depths of the sea, whose bottom was unknown to men. Some believed the waters flowed from an abyss far beneath the Earth. In scripture, the bottomless pit is defined as a chamber located somewhere under the crust of the Earth where certain spirits are bound. It is the location where Satan will be chained for a thousand years (Rev. 20:1-2).

One day the abyss will awaken to release hot magma as ancient inactive volcanoes are energized, sending billowing smoke into the skies above the once peaceful mountain cones. Coastal lands will shake with earthquakes, shift tectonic plates under the sea, and create movement of the Earth, followed by tsunamis.

In John's vision of the Great Tribulation, he saw an angel with a key unlock a shaft of the bottomless pit. Immediately, plumes of black smoke arose from inside the Earth, enough smoke to darken the sun and the air (Rev. 9:1-2). From the smoke came strange creatures that John described as locusts, which will be given power like scorpions to torment people for five months who do not have the seal of God in their foreheads.

In the book of Revelation, John saw and named the demonic angelic king that will oversee this horde of underworld creatures:

> "And they had as king over them the angel of the bottomless pit, whose name in Hebrew is Abaddon, but in Greek he has the name Apollyon."
>
> – Revelation 9:11 (NKJV)

Abaddon and Apollyon have the same meaning, "destruction or destroyer, one who brings death." This king spirit brings forth death and destruction. Recall in the book of Exodus that God released an angel who slew the firstborn sons and animals in Egypt, and He called the angel "the destroyer." The Hebrew root can also refer to something that will decay or something that is set to be ruined because of this angel's visitation. (Exod. 12:23).

God has angels that are assigned to initiate a judgment of sudden death. Another such example is the angel of the Lord that struck dead 185,000 Assyrian troops in one night (2 Kings 19:35). In Acts chapter 5, Ananias and Sapphira were struck dead after Satan filled their hearts to lie to the Holy Spirit. Acts 12:23 reveals that an angel of the Lord struck Herod, and he died after being eaten by worms.

In the Apocalypse, moving from Revelation chapters 9 to 17, John penned an unusual verse that again mentions the bottomless pit:

> "The beast that you saw was, and is not, and will ascend out of the bottomless pit and go to perdition. And those who dwell on

> *the earth will marvel, whose names are not written in the Book of Life from the foundation of the world, when they see the beast that was, and is not, and yet is."*
>
> – Revelation 17:8 (NKJV)

In the 1,900-plus years since John wrote that verse, many theories have emerged to explain the meaning of "the beast was, and is not, and will ascend from the abyss." In chapter 17, John saw a harlot riding a beast (the beast is the Antichrist kingdom; see Revelation 13:1-2) with seven heads and ten horns. This woman is linked to the False Prophet and a false religion whose city is destroyed in Revelation 18 by the ten kings who are following the Antichrist. These ten kings had no kingdom or authority until they were given authority and power in the Antichrist's new kingdom (see Rev. 17:12).

There is one major prophetic empire and one of the dragon's seven heads that once was, did not exist in John's day, and will ascend from the pit of darkness. That is the ancient prince of Babylon. In Revelation 9, four angels are bound under the Euphrates River and are loosed on the earth for a year, a month, and a day. They will successfully organize a two-hundred-million-man army that will cause death to a third of the human population (Rev. 9:15).

If this prince spirit ascending from the abyss is one of the heads (empires) that was wounded unto death and arises in the Middle East to form a new Babylonian center of power, then this spirit will lead the Antichrist and his confederation to *perdition* (Rev. 17:8, 11). That Greek word is *apoleian* and it means "utter destruction."

THE ANTICHRIST AND THREE EVIL SPIRITS

John observed several key events happening during the Great Tribulation. Among them, he saw unclean demonic spirits that will be involved in emerging developments during the last forty-two months of the tribulation. John wrote:

> "Then the sixth angel poured out his bowl on the great river Euphrates, and its water was dried up, so that the way of the kings from the east might be prepared. And I saw three unclean spirits like frogs coming out of the mouth of the dragon, out of the mouth of the beast, and out of the mouth of the false prophet. For they are spirits of demons, performing signs, which go out to the kings of the earth and of the whole world, to gather them to the battle of that great day of God Almighty."
>
> – REVELATION 16:12-14 (NKJV)

Four demonic angels are presently confined at the Euphrates River (Rev. 9:14), which will eventually become a dried riverbed during the tribulation. This allows the kings to march from eastern nations, across the dried Euphrates, to the area of ancient Babylon, Iran, Syria, Lebanon, and Israel.

Three unclean spirits take full possession of the Antichrist, the beast (the ten kings), and the False Prophet. Certain early civilizations associated frogs with fertility and rebirth. In the days of ancient Israel, the Egyptians worshipped a frog goddess that they named Heqet. The reason for frog worship was that frogs appeared after the Nile flooded, and the flooded Nile helped regenerate the soil. Egyptians correlated the frogs with flooding and regenerated soil, which brought fertile crops. Therefore, they believed frogs should be worshipped.

The Euphrates River begins in eastern Turkey and eventually empties into the Persian Gulf. This was a primary source of water for animals and agriculture in early Mesopotamia. When the Euphrates River goes dry, the false frog gods should have power to restore the waters of the Euphrates, which will not happen, of course.

Instead, these three frog-like spirits will control the mouths—that is, the words and speeches—of the Antichrist, the False Prophet, and the ten kings. They also will have the authority to perform false miracles. These are the three primary satanic powers—a satanic trinity—working together to empower this trio of destruction.

Scripture indicates there are three evil powers at work:

- Satan himself (Rev. 13:4)

- the king spirit of the bottomless pit (Rev. 9:11)

- the angel of a former kingdom that ascends from the abyss (Rev. 17:8).

Satan works directly with the Antichrist. The beast from the bottomless pit aligns with the ten kings to form an eighth kingdom that appoints the Antichrist as their leader. The False Prophet is the third actor who will be given power to do false miracles and deceive those who dwell on the earth (Rev. 13:14). Satan is called the "god of this world" who blinds the minds of those who do not believe (2 Cor. 4:4), and he is called the "prince of the power of the air" (Eph. 2:2). In this satanic tribulation trinity, Satan sets himself up in the temple in Jerusalem, proclaiming himself to be God (2 Thess. 2:4). The Antichrist's right-hand man is the False Prophet, whom John sees with two horns like a lamb (Rev. 13:11-12), thereby taking on the same symbolism of Christ, who is identified as "the Lamb of God" (John 1:29, 36). Satan uses the Great Tribulation as an opportunity to mock God and Christ.

The eventual opening of the abyss that John wrote about in Revelation 9 will be the beginning of the end for those living on the earth during this time. This is why that season is called the Great Tribulation (Matt. 24:21).

CHAPTER 9

THE PEOPLE OF THE BEAST MEET THE LION IN BASHAN

One end-time prophetic event is presently being discussed and taught by biblically aware Christians, Jewish Rabbis, and even some Muslims. It is the war of Gog of Magog, recorded by Ezekiel in chapters 38 and 39.

When we analyze details of Ezekiel 38 and 39 for a proper interpretation, many clues can be uncovered. The first point to consider is the location where invading armies will cross into Israel's borders. Ezekiel 38:19 speaks of Bashan, a place mentioned around sixty times in the Old Testament. Bashan is located in northeastern Israel, and it borders Lebanon and Syria.

Biblical Bashan includes the area of the modern Golan Heights. Golan is used four times in the Old Testament, but it refers to a city in the Bashan area—Golan in Bashan. The Golan Heights (Bashan) has miles and miles of lush fertile land, green hills, and a thriving agricultural community. From the high point at the Crusader-era castle ruins known as Nimrod's Fortress, one can see Mount Hermon, Syria, Lebanon, the Hula Valley, and the Galilee hills. It is one of the most beautiful parts of Israel.

The Hebrew word Golan (gola) means *exile, captive, to be carried away*. In Moses' time, this area was home to a giant named Og, king of Bashan, whose bed was close to fourteen feet long and six feet wide (Deut. 3:11). The early giants were widely known, and they kept people in bondage, fear, and captivity. Perhaps this is why the region was given the name Golan.

Before the 1967 Six-Day War, the Bashan area was part of Syria. When Holy Land tourists ride the bus up the hills of Bashan, they can see rusty barbed wire fencing with faded signs warning not to cross the area. Nearly sixty years later, there still could be landmines scattered underground in unpopulated areas. Tourists can also visit military bunkers, constructed with poured concrete or stacked stones, that once housed Syrian soldiers before the 1967 conflict.

After the war, Israel annexed the Golan Heights. Six years later, on Yom Kippur, October 6, 1973, Syria launched a surprise attack in the north to try to reclaim the Golan Heights. (At the same time, Egypt attacked in the south to reclaim the Sinai Peninsula, which they had lost in the same 1967 war.)

Both Syria and Egypt failed to meet their goals, and the war ended on October 25 after a U.N. brokered ceasefire. Israel annexed the Golan Heights in 1981, but Syria still claims it. (Egypt regained the Sinai Peninsula later through negotiations.)

An important water source for Israel is in the Bashan - Golan Heights area where three headwaters of the Jordan River converge. Half of the water that flows into the Jordan River comes from the Dan River at the foothills of Mount Hermon. Even the Sea of Galilee, Israel's largest freshwater lake, receives water from the Jordan River. Syria, most Palestinians and Arab nations, and in fact, most of the world except for the United States, refuses to accept Israel's annexation of the Golan Heights. They believe that Israel is occupying the land, which is currently home to Jews, Druze, and a minority of Arabs.

The second area of intense fighting in the Gog of Magog War is described as happening at the east side of the northern part of the Dead Sea, as the following passage in Ezekiel indicates:

> *"And it shall come to pass in that day, that I will give unto Gog a place there of graves in Israel, the valley of the passengers on the east of the sea: and it shall stop the noses of the passengers: and there shall they bury Gog and all his multitude: and they shall call it The Valley of Hamon-gog."*
>
> – Ezekiel 39:11 (KJV)

Several details can be derived from this verse. The sea refers to the Dead Sea in Israel—called the Salt Sea in the Torah—which is not actually a sea, but a large saltwater lake that is ten times saltier than the Mediterranean Sea. The Dead Sea is gradually receding because it is no longer well fed by sources such as the Jordan River, as most of the water from the Jordan runoff has been diverted to other areas for agricultural use. Currently, the Dead Sea is thirty-one miles long and nine miles across at its widest point. The west side of the Dead Sea borders Israel, with the northwestern portion bordering the area in Israel referred to as the West Bank. The eastern shore of the Dead Sea borders Jordan.

The "valley of the passengers" mentioned by Ezekiel is geographically located in Moab, which is modern-day Jordan. The Hebrew name for the valley, Emek ha-Avrim, indicates this was a known passageway between the mountains in Moab where travelers could cross over near the northern Dead Sea into Jericho. On the Jordanian side, the passage is located near Mount Nebo, where Moses viewed the Promised Land before he died.

In Ezekiel's vision, he saw the bodies of Israel's enemies piled up along this valley of the passengers for miles and miles. The prophet noted that there were so many, the sheer number of rotting bodies would stop anyone from attempting to pass through the valley. The prophet mentions the troops of Gog being buried in this valley, and that it would be named the Valley of Hamon-gog.

The reason for the battle ensuing on the *east side of the sea* may be linked to the Jordan Valley. From the north end of the Dead Sea, if a traveler continues north in the Jordan Valley, he will arrive at Tiberius on the western shore of the Sea of Galilee (Lake Kinneret). The Galilee region is a lush green area where all kinds of fruits and vegetables are grown. However, the amount of land for agriculture is limited because Israel is a small country and much of it, such as the Negev desert and the Judean Wilderness—is dry, rugged, and rocky. In the harsh desert of southern Israel where food is grown, irrigation and other water systems are required to provide water.

To further complicate matters, the entire Middle East is one of the driest regions on Earth, with seventy percent of the land being arid or semi-arid. Water quickly becomes scarce, and water access has been and will continue to be a political issue.

According to biblical prophecies, global food shortages will occur in the future. The Jordan Valley is an agricultural treasure, along with the entire Galilee region north of Tiberius. The value of Israel's agricultural land is enhanced by the fact that they have developed the most advanced water technologies in the world, including desalinization that turns sea water into fresh water. They have developed several successful methods to deal with water shortages.

A PROPHETIC NUGGET HERE

There is another important prophetic nugget concealed in Ezekiel's vision. As mentioned, before the 1967 war, Bashan (the Golan Heights) was part of Syria. Yet, Ezekiel indicated that when this war occurs, Israel will be in control of Bashan and will be dwelling safely in villages without walls (Ezek. 38:11). This simple fact indicates that the

Gog of Magog prophecy did not and could not have occurred before Israel gained control of the Bashan. That did not happen until 1967.

A second point is the phrase *east of the sea*. At the time of the 1967 war, Jordan controlled the northern part of the Dead Sea, because they had annexed the area following the 1948 war. After June of 1967, Jordan lost control and Israel gained the land, including East Jerusalem, Hebron, Bethlehem, Jericho, and Qumran. The entire west side of the Dead Sea was now under Israel's jurisdiction. Thus, 1967 was a major prophetic marker, as Israel gained from Syria and Jordan the very two areas where the Ezekiel invaders will perish—the Golan Heights and the valley of passengers north of the Dead Sea.

PERSIA'S INVOLVEMENT

Persia is a name mentioned in twenty-seven verses in the Old Testament. Another biblical name for a section of Persia is Elam, which was primarily southwestern Persia (Iran) and it bordered the modern area of southern Iraq. With Elam being part of Persia that is now known as Iran, notice this Elam prediction in Ezekiel:

> "There is Elam and all her multitude round about her grave, all of them slain, fallen by the sword, which are gone down uncircumcised into the nether parts of the earth, which caused their terror in the land of the living; yet have they borne their shame with them that go down to the pit."
>
> – Ezekiel 32:24 (KJV)

In chapter 32, Ezekiel mentioned terror seven times (Ezekiel 32:23-27; 30, 32). In the same chapter, the prophet lists nations that instigate terror, including Elam. He described the multitudes of Elam fallen by the sword—a biblical allusion to war. This could be a regional war or a larger part of the Gog of Magog military campaign, when according to Ezekiel 39:2 (King James translation), God will destroy five-sixths of the invading armies on the mountains of Israel.

In chapter 32, Ezekiel speaks of men who terrorize Israel and other nations. When they are slain, their souls descend into hell, identified here as the "nether parts of the earth," which is the underworld area for departed lost souls. These terrorists "go down to the pit," which is the pit of hell that is presently under the Earth's crust. This will become their prison of damnation, as all unrepentant murderers will spend eternity in the lake of fire (Rev. 21:8).

Ezekiel also listed Meshech and Tubal as two geographical regions participating in the Gog of Magog war (Ezek. 38:2). Gog is mentioned as the "chief prince of Meshech and Tubal," places that most believe are identified today as part of modern Turkey. Ezekiel said Meshech and Tubal are also terrors to the nations (Ezek. 32:26).

Under leadership of the Ottoman Empire, from 1299 to 1922, millions of people were slain. The Ottomans captured many countries and committed genocide against groups such as the Greeks, Assyrians, and Armenians, killing as many as one and a half million Armenian Christians. By the year 1520, the Ottoman Empire had conquered so many people and obtained so much land that the empire covered 1.3 million square miles.

The Elamites, that is, some of the people in modern Iran, have supported Hamas, Hezbollah, Yemen, ISIS, and other terrorist groups who strike Israel, terrorize the Jews with missiles, and even terrorize their own people. Iran has struck Israel by launching hundreds of missiles in one night under the cover of darkness. Moses penned a promise of protection from night arrows:

> *"You shall not be afraid of the terror by night, nor of the arrow that flies by day"*
>
> – PSALM 91:5 (NKJV)

In Moses' time, arrows were shot from a bow, which was once a common war weapon. In modern times, the Arrow is a ballistic missile defense system developed by Israel.

During the Gulf War, Iraq shot Scud ballistic missiles into Israel. I discussed this with a Jewish rabbi who expressed his opinion that, since Iraq is the land of ancient Babylon, a prophecy by Jeremiah may have a parallel with the war against Iraq. He read Jeremiah 51:11, "Make bright the arrows; gather the shields…" The rabbi believed this could allude to the Arrow missile defense system being used to intercept these Scud missiles.

Another recently used Israeli missile interception system is called "David's Sling." David wrote many of the Psalms and is also recognized as a prophet who sometimes saw the future (Acts 2:29-30). He wrote: "Yea, he sent out his arrows, and scattered them; and he shot out lightnings and discomfited them" (Psalm 18:14 KJV).

When an incoming missile is intercepted, the enemy's missile is blown to pieces and scattered. The impact produces a burst of light and streaks that create the appearance of lightning. The arrows of God *discomfited* the enemy, a Hebrew word meaning, "to disturb, confuse, damage, or destroy." The Hebrew root word can refer to making a loud noise, which does occur once a missile is intercepted.

THE LION PEOPLE

The symbol of the tribe of Judah is a lion. Lions are considered the king of the beasts—strong, courageous, intimidating, and fierce in time of conflict. They move slowly when they are stalking prey, but once they charge, they swiftly take down their target. Micah wrote:

> *"And the remnant of Jacob shall be among the nations in the midst of many peoples like a lion among the beasts of the forest,*

like a young lion [suddenly appearing] among the flocks of sheep which, when it goes through, treads down and tears in pieces, and there is no deliverer. Your hand will be lifted up above your adversaries, and all your enemies shall be cut off."

– MICAH 5:8-9 (AMP)

While on earth, Christ's prophetic symbol was a Lamb who would be slain for the sins of mankind. In heaven, as He prepares to make war with the armies of the world, He is the "Lion of the tribe of Judah" who will prevail (Rev. 5:5).

CHAPTER 10

GOD VERSUS GOG – BIG HOOKS IN LITTLE JAWS

The coalition that will form against Israel in the future includes Iran (Persia). Iran is about one-sixth the size of the United States and almost two-and-a-half times the size of Texas. Iran's population is around ninety million people, and they are said to have 610,000 active troop personnel, plus reserves and paramilitary. Persia is mentioned in Ezekiel as one of the countries that will unite a coalition against Israel. Ezekiel reveals how this will transpire:

> "I will turn you around, put hooks into your jaws, and lead you out, with all your army, horses, and horsemen, all splendidly clothed, a great company with bucklers and shields, all of them handling swords. Persia, Ethiopia, and Libya are with them, all of them with shield and helmet; Gomer and all its troops; the house of Togarmah from the far north and all its troops—many people are with you."
>
> – Ezekiel 38:4-6 (NKJV)

The meaning of the term "hooks into your jaws" has been analyzed and debated for generations. Perhaps it is simply a metaphor explaining that God will *force* the armies to descend against Israel, without their knowledge that the evil plan is a divine setup for their own destruction

(Ezek. 38:10). Or perhaps the phrase holds a hint of something deeper.

There have been so many different interpretive opinions of "hooks into your jaws" since I began preaching in the 1970s. One early theory suggested that the hooks to bring the armies down was the mineral wealth of the Dead Sea. This idea was based primarily on the fact that the battle will happen on the east side of the Dead Sea. Another suggestion was that the hook will be an oil discovery in Israel that will stir jealousy among the Gulf States' oil producers. I reject both theories for different reasons.

Persia is a wealthy nation with an abundance of oil and other resources that generate plenty of income each year, with oil exports alone delivering over sixty billion dollars a year. Some oil sheiks in the Gulf states have so much wealth, they cannot spend it fast enough. Israel, on the other hand, has natural gas offshore, but they have very little oil, other than olive oil.

Note that the hooks are in the jaws, and this affects all the nations listed, not just one. God referenced jaws, when He could have said that He would put a ring in their nose, a yoke on their neck, or a rope to drag them into conflict. When I think of jaws, I think of food, because it takes the strength of jaws to chew food. This could conceal the reason for the nations coming into Israel, thinking they can access Israel's food supplies and take possession of a million acres of farmland.

This could also hint that a severe food crisis has struck the invading nations, and they falsely believe they can overpower Israel in a ground war. Ezekiel said the invaders come to take spoil (possessions), including gold (wealth), cattle, and goods (Ezek. 38:12-13). What scenarios, besides severe drought and weather conditions, could cause such food disruptions among the invading nations?

ENVIRONMENTAL TERRORISM

On June 14, 2025, I preached several services in Knoxville, Tennessee. As I was resting and praying after one of the services, I began to hear words that I had never heard before. I grabbed my phone and searched for a word I was hearing. To my shock, it meant environmental terrorism. I looked up environmental terrorism, and it is defined as destruction or threat of destruction of the environment by groups or individuals. It involves violence, force, release of biological agents, contamination of water supplies, deliberate modification of the environment, and the list goes on. This is often done for the purpose of advancing political or social agendas.

Environmental terrorism can include sabotage attacks on infrastructure such as oil, fuel transportation, rivers, and reservoirs. It includes intentionally set fires that burn thousands of acres of forest, such as we have seen in the United States and in Israel when one or more people retaliate by burning the beautiful, forested hills and destroying homes in the process. The commission of the act of sabotage and ecological terrorism is called ecotage.

Environmental terrorism, or ecotage, could also be used by terrorists to disrupt nations by destroying food distribution centers, poisoning water supplies, and destroying agricultural products. When I heard the word, I sensed this was possibly a warning of some type of future attack on important U.S. or allied infrastructure that could also impact food supplies or distribution. These people often operate undetected, and some damage could be accomplished from the inside or by expert hackers shutting down communications or other vital systems required to operate the infrastructure.

THE KURDS AND POISONED WATER

When Saddam Hussein was president of Iraq, he used chemical nerve agents and mustard gas forty times against the Kurds in northern Iraq. The deadliest attack in modern history occurred in the Kurdish city of Halabja, where up to five thousand people died and ten thousand more suffered long term or permanent injuries.

I talked to a man in Israeli military circles who sat in a meeting where Saddam's attack against the Kurds was discussed. He said the Israelis had received intelligence that Saddam had a chemical weapon that could be placed in water to poison a water supply, and he had tested it on a small community of Kurds by placing it in their village well water. The intelligence Israel obtained indicated that the entire village of about four hundred people were killed by drinking from the poisoned well. There was concern that this would be weaponized on a larger scale and placed in a town or city drinking water supply.

IRAN AND ECO-TERRORISM

I want to make clear that the following is hypothetical, but it does align with the idea of "hooks in the jaws."

Iran has nuclear power plants that require uranium. Intelligence reports indicated that Iranian nuclear scientists had also been enriching uranium, enough that Iran had the ability to build up to ten nuclear weapons.

The Russian people understand what happens to a city when one nuclear power plant leaks radioactive material. On April 26, 1986, an improper safety test was conducted on a nuclear plant at Chernobyl, and the resulting explosions and fire released a large cloud of radioactive material into the atmosphere. Thirty employees at the plant died, and hundreds of thousands of people in the area were forced to relocate after being exposed to radiation that resulted in long term health effects, such as thyroid cancer and birth defects.

Radioactive emissions that leak into the ground make the area uninhabitable. When it leaks into soil and water, it causes the water to become undrinkable and the soil to become too toxic for growing food. Depending on the type of radiation, it could take a few weeks, two hundred years, or thousands of years for the radioactive isotopes to decay and the site to be safe again.

If Iran continues its nuclear program, the possibility exists that it could place their food supply in jeopardy. First, there could be an accident, similar to that experienced at Chernobyl. Iran has one active commercial power plant on the coast of the Persian Gulf at Bushehr, which is located 465 miles from the capital of Tehran. If a Chernobyl-type accident occurred at the Bushehr plant, the immediate danger zone is a six-mile radius, and people must evacuate immediately. The wider fallout zone could reach three hundred miles or more, depending on wind direction and speed, topography, rainfall, and other factors.

Iran also has other nuclear facilities: Natanz, an enrichment facility located 135 miles from Tehran; Fordow, buried under a mountain sixty miles from Tehran; Arak, a heavy water reactor located 155 miles from Tehran; Isfahan Nuclear Technology Center located 215 miles from Tehran; and the Tehran Research Reactor located in Tehran. Natanz, Fordow, Arak, and Isfahan were destroyed in the 2025 conflict between Iran and Israel.

Iranian leaders state that they will not stop uranium enrichment, and they voted to suspend cooperation with the International Atomic Energy Agency, which is an international nuclear watchdog. Nobody knows what Iran's leaders might decide to do in the next few years. But if a serious accident or high Richter scale earthquake happened in the area, it is not unreasonable to think that a high population city like Tehran, as well as food supplies, could be affected.

Modern nuclear facilities, although not indestructible, are built to withstand earthquakes. However, the Japanese Fukushima plant failed and partially melted down because of a tsunami that followed a 9.0 earthquake in 2011. Radiation was released into the water, soil, and air, and cleanup is estimated to take decades.

Another possibility is that Iran continues to enrich uranium and again develops or acquires enough enriched uranium to build nuclear weapons. The 2025 bombings of their facilities likely will not stop future production. It merely set things back for a while. If Iran's leaders choose to enrich uranium again, that triggers the possibility that Iran will one day use nuclear weapons in the Middle East and create a chaotic situation that affects food and water supplies.

Such theoretical scenarios help us understand how Iran or any other rogue nation that eventually joins the Gog of Magog invasion of Israel could fulfill the "hooks in the jaws" prophecy after causing food supplies to greatly diminish. A united coalition will use ground troops to enter the two areas where most food supplies and farmland are located, and farmland is often a spoil of war.

Of course, other severe problems can cause food shortages as well. Drought, blight, floods, and persistent severe weather can impact crops. In the last fifty years, Iran has experience agricultural shortages caused by weather and drought.

As this book was being written, Iran was experiencing its fifth straight year of drought, and the country is said to be on the verge of an environmental collapse. They are nearly out of water. The blame is being placed, not just on drought, but on decades of mismanagement and an obsession with regional conflicts. The Iranian government could have used their money to improve their agricultural and water infrastructure, but instead they used it to fund and train terrorists throughout the Middle East.

Most of Iran's farms are no larger than twenty-four acres. They grow grains such as wheat, barley, and rice. They grow a variety of fruits, vegetables, lentils, chickpeas, and pistachios. About one-third of their land is suitable for farming, but not all of that is cultivated. Soil quality is poor, and of course, water is scarce. Sources say that agriculture uses ninety-two percent of the fresh water in Iran, and the country doesn't have the kind of technology for farming and water resources that Israel has developed.

Israel's farming technology both conserves water and brings water to arid places such as the desert regions, fulfilling the Isaiah 35:1 prophecy that "the desert shall rejoice and blossom like a rose." In some places, agricultural produce is harvested two or even three times a year, all because of advanced technology. Avocados, dates, citrus fruits, peppers, tomatoes, olive oil, and wine are some of the products Israel exports. This fulfills the Isaiah 27:6 prophecy that "Israel shall blossom and bud, and fill the face of the world with fruit."

However, the nations that surround Israel have not focused on improving agricultural techniques to ease potential threats of famine.

THE FOOD SHORTAGES COME IMMEDIATELY

If, as some suggest, the war of Gog of Magog unfolds prior to the Rapture, or as others teach, near the beginning of the seven-year treaty of Daniel 9:27 and the Great Tribulation (Matt. 24:21; Rev. 7:14), then food shortages will happen right away. In Revelation 6, in the early part of the Great Tribulation, there will be food rationing that causes prices to spiral out of control, with bread costing an entire day's wage. Following are the troubles associated with the four horsemen that are released upon the earth at the beginning of the tribulation:

- Barley and wheat will be rationed (Rev. 6:5-6).

- One-fourth of the world's population will die through sword, famine, and pestilence (Rev. 6:8).
- The beasts of the field (animals) will turn on people and kill them (Rev. 6:8).

Unless you grow food in your own backyard, growing fruits, vegetables, and grains is only the first phase of the food distribution process. If the food products cannot be harvested and delivered for distribution, then people cannot obtain the food to eat. War can halt food harvesting and distribution for several reasons, all of which make farm-to-table distribution next to impossible. Natural disasters can destroy fields of crops, processing and distribution centers, and methods of transportation. If food in the fields cannot be harvested, it will rot and return to the earth. Extended wars will eventually affect the water and food supply. In Revelation 6, two of the four horsemen are carrying swords, which is a symbol of war and conflict.

In the future, an asteroid will strike the earth and poison a portion of the rivers and waters:

> *"And the third angel sounded, and there fell a great star from heaven, burning as it were a lamp, and it fell upon the third part of the rivers, and upon the fountains of waters; And the name of the star is called Wormwood: and the third part of the waters became wormwood; and many men died of the waters, because they were made bitter."*
>
> – REVELATION 8:10-11 (KJV)

People cannot survive long without food and especially drinking water. Wars, advanced weapons and nuclear devices, radiation that pollutes the land, and many other tragic events could hinder farming, harvesting, and food transportation.

Regardless of the causes, food shortages and famines have the potential to bring out a mob mentality. Theft, breaking and entering, and even harming their own friends to survive will become commonplace during that time. Today, when food is shipped to war-torn countries that experience shortages, often the supplies are stolen by government leaders or the military, then sold on the black market.

Famine conditions in certain Middle Eastern countries could become so severe that people will be convinced they have a justifiable reason to invade Israel and take over food supplies to feed their own people. I contend that the "hooks in the jaws" will include a dire need for food and water, and that the Gog of Magog invasion will focus on the need for food, farmland, and fresh water.

CHAPTER 11

CAN THE ANTICHRIST OVERTAKE A MILITARILY ARMED ISRAEL?

In the early years of its independence, the state of Israel was outnumbered militarily in many of the wars and confrontations with surrounding long-established neighboring countries. First they fought the War of Independence in 1948, immediately after the state of Israel was established. Then came the Sinai Campaign of 1956, the Six-Day War in 1967, the Yom Kippur War of 1973, and other troubles in between.

Since then, Israel has built a strong military with powerful weapons. With a few exceptions, military service is mandatory for both men and women upon reaching age eighteen. Around 170 countries maintain active armed forces that vary in size, strength, ability, and funding. The 2025 Global Firepower index, which ranks military strength of 145 world powers, gives the United States, Russia, and China top ranking, while Israel is rated 15th and Iran is 16th.

Despite its 15th place ranking, Israel clearly has a military advantage through advanced technologies and intelligence services. Considering Israel's capabilities and the fact that God has supernaturally intervened on their behalf in nearly every war, we might look at Ezekiel's vision of this future Gog of Magog invasion of Israel, along with the final battle of Armageddon, and wonder how it will be possible for these nations to invade and overcome such a powerful military. How will it be possible for the Antichrist and his ten-nation coalition to seize Jerusalem and set up a global command and religious center for himself and the False Prophet without a successful resistance from the Israeli military?

Israel and Jerusalem were part of God's divine plan from the foundation of the world. The Almighty initiated an everlasting covenant with Abraham, the father of a future Hebrew nation that would be named after Jacob, whose name God changed to Israel (Gen. 32:28). King David captured the stronghold of Jebus, naming the hill (about 12 acres) the city of David (2 Sam. 5:7, 1 Chron. 11:4), also called Mount Zion (Psa. 48:2). Later David purchased Mount Moriah, a threshing floor owned by a Jebusite, thus marking the spot for God's sacred Temple to be built by David's son, Solomon.

Jerusalem has been the center of political and spiritual conflict for three thousand years. Some calculate that Jerusalem has been besieged twenty-three times, captured and recaptured forty-four times, attacked fifty-two times, and destroyed twice. In the historical geo-political context, Jerusalem (and Israel itself) should not exist as they do today.

This enduring city of stone should be listed among the silent ruins of other ancient cities of antiquity, including most of the cities mentioned by John in Revelation chapters 2 and 3. All seven cities were thriving business and trade centers of their day. Only Smyrna, currently named Izmir, is a large, modern city in Turkey today. Thyatira and Philadelphia, having been renamed Akhisar and Alaşehir, are small towns, and the other four are ruins and tourist sites. They are a shadow of what once was, a story of a bygone era.

In contrast, Israel and Jerusalem, a land that hosts three monotheistic religions that each hold claim to the spiritual significance of Jerusalem, is a sought-after tourist destination that blends ancient history with contemporary culture. People can enjoy the Mediterranean coastline and modern cities, while visiting ancient, excavated sites where important historical events took place, and where one culture disappeared, and another was built atop its ruins. With Jerusalem's history of conflict, one would expect the city to be a pile of limestone ashlars, where tour guides recall the glory of the past, and tourists can carry home rocks and a vial of holy dirt.

From a biblical perspective, the reasons for Jerusalem's protection and endurance are fourfold:

1. God will not break His covenant nor alter the word which comes out of His mouth (Psa. 89:34). God made an eternal oath to Abraham that a great nation and many nations would proceed from him (Gen. 17:5-6). Israel began with Abraham, and by the time of the Hebrew Exodus from Egypt, there were twelve tribes and 600,000 footmen (Num. 11:21). Generations after Abraham, God made a covenant with King David that His seed would rule from Jerusalem (Psalm 89:3-4; 2 Sam. 7:12-16). Today, Israel and Jerusalem have an everlasting agreement with God that cannot be broken. God is the everlasting Father who will not break a covenant, and He can never be overthrown.

2. According to scripture, Michael the archangel stands guard over Israel. In Daniel 12:1, Daniel called Michael "the great prince" who stands up for the children of Israel in her day of trouble. Michael is given authority to confront Satan face-to-face and thwart Satan's purposes (Jude 9; Rev. 12:7-10). A Jewish remnant will be spared from annihilation during the Great Tribulation, because Michael will be involved in Israel's defense and protection to ensure the Jewish remnant's survival until the return of Christ the Messiah to set up His kingdom.

3. God calls Jerusalem "My holy mountain" (Isa. 65:25), "the mountain of the LORD of hosts" (Zech. 8:3), and "the city of the great King" (Psa. 48:2). God said that whoever

touches Israel and Jerusalem "touches the apple of His eye" (Zech. 2:8). The "apple" does not refer to a physical apple. In Hebrew it is a metaphor referring to the pupil of the eye, and it speaks of something that is treasured and to be protected. God is saying that He is very sensitive to the way nations or individuals treat Jerusalem and Israel. We are told, "Pray for the peace of Jerusalem: May they prosper who love you" (Psa. 122:6).

4. The Messiah will rule from Jerusalem! During the thousand-year reign of Christ, His earthy living quarters will be at a newly constructed Temple compound on the Temple Mount in Jerusalem. Ezekiel chapters 44 – 48 describe this Temple in minute detail. Jerusalem is called "the eternal city" for a reason. It is interesting that Rome, Italy is also called "the eternal city," but Rome has experienced only ten to fifteen major attacks throughout its history, which is nothing compared to Jerusalem. The city of Jerusalem is where Christ was crucified, buried, raised from the dead, ascended, and will again return. Christ's rule on earth from Israel and Jerusalem, as King of kings, ensures the endurance of Israel, Jerusalem, and God's covenant people.

The future war of Gog of Magog, the tribulation wars, and the mother of all military battles, the campaign called Armageddon, are all designed in the war room of darkness for the purpose of erasing the memory of the Jews and Israel from the face of the earth. From God's perspective, Israel's survival in all future wars of flesh and blood is due to the Almighty's sovereign protection, which eventually opens the door for the "kingdoms of this world to become the kingdoms of our Lord and of His Christ" (Rev. 11:15).

HOW CAN THE ANTICHRIST DO IT?

The question I have mused upon that people seldom discuss is, how can the Antichrist successfully invade Jerusalem, the capital of Israel, when Israel can protect itself (as recently proven) and initiate deadly assaults on terrorists, militias, or nations who make war against them? When the Antichrist arises, the nations will ask, "Who is able to make war with him?" (Rev. 13:4). The answer is found in searching the scriptures and combining line upon line and precept upon precept (Isa. 28:10):

- The Antichrist will build a strong, Middle East coalition with combined militaries under his authority. The present population of Israel is over nine and a half million, including Arab Palestinians. The population of sixteen Middle Eastern Arab countries, including Iran (which is not Arab), is around 475 million. Many of those countries are considered either enemies or unfriendly toward Israel, and Israeli relations with any of them could turn quickly. If the Arab nations joined a formidable coalition, it would be like a salmon taking on a grizzly bear. With ten nations—many of which will be Islamic—joining the Antichrist, Israel will find itself completely overwhelmed by the numbers.

- There will be an undetermined number of Jews *missing* from Israel during this time known as "Jacob's trouble" (Jer. 30:7). When the gathering together known as the Rapture occurs, the Messianic Jews will be taken to be with the Lord. Later in the tribulation, 144,000 Jewish men will be sealed with the seal of God, then caught up to the heavenly Mount Zion (see Revelation 14). There also will be a large gathering of Jewish people who take flight into the wilderness of Moab (Jordan), to a place that many believe will be the natural rock fortification of Petra, where they will be protected from the Antichrist invasion for two reasons. First, the nation of Jordan, called "Edom, Moab, and the chief children of Ammon" in the book of Daniel, will escape the control of the Antichrist (see Dan. 11:41). Second, God Himself supernaturally protects this Jewish remnant from Satan's destructive plans. Therefore, by the time the Antichrist makes his move to Jerusalem, a reduced number of Jews will remain.

- A third reason is revealed by Paul. The apostle wrote in 2 Thessalonians chapter 2 concerning the coming of Christ and our gathering together to Him. In this letter, Paul revealed that there is a restrainer that holds back the revealing of the man of sin (the Antichrist). Paul indicated that this restrainer must be removed first, then the wicked one (Antichrist) will be revealed. He calls the restrainer "he," causing many prophetic teachers to believe the restrainer is the Holy Spirit working on earth through the church. Israel, Jerusalem, and the Jewish people there are presently under a protective hedge that restrains the destruction of Israel. Once the Antichrist is revealed, the adversary is given a forty-two-month season to operate unrestrained in his goal of control and destruction. In the end, he loses.

IN SUMMARY

The reasons why the Antichrist can take over Jerusalem when Israel has a strong army, advanced technology, and powerful weaponry is summed up as follows:

1. The number of nations and troops aligning with the Antichrist will far outnumber the military of Israel. That will change at the return of Christ the Messiah who will confront the armies of the world, destroying them with the spirit (breath) of His mouth and the brightness of His coming (2 Thess. 2:8; Rev. 19:15, 21).

2. Presently, the Jewish population of Jerusalem is about sixty percent, while the Muslim population is thirty-seven percent. Israel's current military, with both active personal and reservists, is estimated to be, at the most, 641,500 men and women. With a combination of the sudden return of Christ for His followers, the 144,000 Jewish men who are marked with the seal of God and later caught up to the throne room (Rev. 7 and 14), and another unknown number of Jews fleeing and crossing over into Jordan, the sheer number of enemy troops by comparison will allow the Antichrist to move in. The vast majority of Jerusalem's inhabitants will be Muslims, with a Jewish remnant being assaulted in the western half of the city. Zechariah 14:2 describes this terrible event: "For I will gather all nations against Jerusalem to battle; and the city shall be taken, and

the houses rifled, and the women ravished; and half of the city shall go forth into captivity, and the residue of the people shall not be cut off from the city."

3. In the book of Job, God had placed an invisible, protective hedge around Job's family, his possessions, and his life. Satan noted that he was unable to penetrate the shield that surrounded Job. Only when this invisible, protective wall was temporarily removed was Satan permitted to kill, steal, and destroy, and then for only a limited time. In the end, Job was restored with a double blessing (Job 42:10). This same temporary removal of a shield is seen during the Great Tribulation as well.

Up to now, God has consistently shielded Jerusalem and Israel from major disasters, wars, and plots to destroy them. This restraining power is what Paul alluded to that not only defends Israel, but according to Paul, is withholding the Antichrist from making a move before his appointed season. Religious and political radicals have called for death to the Jews and the control over the land of Israel for thousands of years—from the slavery strongholds of Egyptian pharaohs, to the murderous plot of a demonically inspired Haman in Persia, to the death camps of German Chancellor and Nazi leader Adolph Hitler. Yet from the beginning of time, God has guarded Jerusalem, Israel, and the people.

Jacob's trouble is coming, but Israel will be delivered out of it and thrive again. If the whips on the backs of Egyptian slaves, the iron shackles on exiles headed to Babylon, the ropes and gallows of Haman, and the fires and ashes of the Holocaust could not destroy the Jews, the Antichrist too will suffer utter defeat, when the beast's body is destroyed and given to the eternal burning flame (Dan. 7:11).

CHAPTER 12

THE STRONGEST MIDDLE EASTERN PRINCE SPIRIT ON THE LOOSE

The cosmos is more than stars, nebulas, planets, and gases. It is the passageway from Heaven to Earth for angels. It is a vast battleground above Earth's atmosphere for clashes between angelic forces of good and evil. The faithful angels are continuously exposing and battling decisions being made in the boardroom of the dark kingdom.

In Daniel 10:12-14, God dispatched the archangel Michael to confront this powerful angelic prince operating in the Middle East. Michael engaged this strong demon in face-to-face conflict that I believe continues today with this same entity. Paul identified this wicked spirit as a principality (Eph. 6:12), whose fiery darts can stir up passions of hatred among the religious fanatics in Persia, who hope to weaken and destroy modern Israel.

Various Jewish and Christian writings and traditions place names on God's angels and even on certain demonic entities. Only two of God's angels are mentioned by name in the Bible: Michael and Gabriel, who appear in both testaments. Others are named in deuterocanonical and apocryphal books. There are said to be seven chief angels, each with a specific assignment when dealing with prophecy, healing, miracles, warfare, or answers to prayer. Christian tradition and extra-biblical sources such as the book of Enoch name them as:

- Michael – identified as an archangel, warrior, and defender of Israel

- Gabriel – a messenger angel in both testaments who carried messages to reveal God's plans

- Raphael – mentioned as an angel of healing who stands ready and enters before the glory of the Lord

- Uriel – name means "fire of God;" considered an angel of wisdom and warning

- Raguel – associated with justice

- Saraqael or Sariel – sometimes associated with the execution of God's judgment

- Remiel – associated with hope, faith, and resurrection; leads souls to their judgment.

In Revelation, John noted that in Satan's kingdom, the dragon, a symbol that means a serpent in the Greek language, had seven heads and ten horns. The seven heads can represent the seven nations found in scripture and in prophecy, which includes Egypt, Assyria, Babylon, Media-Persia, Greece, Rome, and the united coalition of nations at the time of the end. Each empire was under the supervision of a strong demonic angel who directed Satan's plots and strategies within those empires.

It is interesting to note that Paul spoke of wrestling against principalities (Eph. 6:12). In the Greek this word can allude to "governments." These spirits are the highest in authority who work in the spirit realm and behind the scenes to raise up leaders—kings, dictators, and evildoers—and inspire them to work against righteousness and propagate wickedness as they attempt to disrupt and hinder God's plans.

Each of these prince spirits took on the name of the very empire to which it was assigned. We observe this in Daniel 10. Daniel was in Babylon when the Persian empire overthrew the Babylonians and seized their city in one night. After the Persian leaders settled in their new Babylonian headquarters, Daniel set aside a season of consecration and prayer for the interpretation of several troubling revelations he had received.

For three weeks, the heavens were as brass, and the voice of God seemed silent. Suddenly on the twenty-first day, he experienced a breakthrough. The angel Gabriel revealed that he was sent to earth on the first day to answer Daniel's prayer, but a demonic angel he called "the prince of the kingdom of Persia" withstood him in the upper atmosphere. This was the same spirit connected to the Media-Persian Empire that had positioned himself over Persia for centuries. Persia (Iran) borders Iraq (the location of Babylon).

When the empires changed leadership from a Babylonian king to a Persian king, the spirit called the prince of Persia transitioned from the Persian palaces to the center of Babylon, where Daniel had lived in royal residences for over seventy years. Daniel was a highly respected and appointed leader in Babylon and was known for his wisdom and ability to interpret dreams, visions, and strange handwriting on the wall. This new prince of Persia knew that Daniel would be a pivotal person to influence the new Persian leaders. Josephus mentioned that, when Darius became the leader of the new empire, Daniel showed a scroll of his vision revealing that the Babylonians would be overthrown by the Persian bear, and how the new kings were fulfilling the prophetic visions. This impressed the king, and he allowed Daniel to live and be a part of his new administration.

ANOTHER GREEK PRINCIPALITY WOULD TAKE OVER

Gabriel provided details of the future war coming to Jerusalem, the Jews, and Israel, including the rise of a man who would eventually capture Jerusalem and create trouble such as never was since the beginning of a nation (Dan. 12:1). This heavenly messenger also revealed a future kingdom that decades later would overthrow the Persians. The angel said, "When I am gone forth (finished with the Persian government), then the prince of Greece will come (Dan. 10:20). This transition happened about two hundred years later, when the Macedonian General Alexander the Great organized a fierce army.

While historians differ on the number of troops Alexander had, there is no question they were highly trained, disciplined and unified, and they operated well under Alexander's leadership. They fought unlike anything the Persian soldiers had ever seen. The Persians surrendered to Alexander, and he moved his administrative headquarters to Babylon.

This demonic prince had been active in Macedonia, which was west of Babylon. The prince of Greece moved his position from Macedonia to Babylon, as indicated by Gabriel. The Persian prince was displaced by this new Grecian prince, and likely went back to the land of Persia during the Greek rule in Babylon.

Seeing there was a high level principality operating in the Persian and Grecian empires (two of the seven heads of the dragon), it stands to reason there is a prince of Egypt, one over the Assyrian kingdom, one behind the Babylonian rulers, and one that centuries later was connected to Rome. These prince spirits make up the heads of the dragon, as these spirits have dominated all six of these historic empires. The final coalition of the Antichrist and his ten kings is called the eighth kingdom, and it emerges from the territory of the previous empires, from Egypt to Rome.

THE RISE OF THE PERSIAN PRINCE

Prior to 1979, the Persian people in Iran were ruled by the Shah of Iran, who was friendly toward the west and the Jews. As mentioned, controversy developed between the Shah and Iran's strict Shi'ite religious leaders over the embrace of western values and the conflict with sharia law. A revolution resulted in the Shah going into exile and a theocracy taking his place, with the Ayatollah becoming the supreme leader and spiritual authority. Islamic students loyal to the revolution and the Ayatollah seized the American embassy in Tehran and held fifty-two Americans hostage for 444 days. The U.S. attempt to rescue the hostages turned into a military disaster for the Carter administration. The hostages were released on January 20, 1981, the day Ronald Reagan was inaugurated as President. Reagan threatened war if the hostages were not released, and they were. Since 1979, Persia has been a center of controversy.

The influence of Iran's new Shi'ite Islamic regime gradually changed the political dynamics of the Middle East. The theocratic Shi'ite regime, with their strict adherence to radical Islamic beliefs, became religious and political enemies of both Israel and the United States. They started supporting and funding any terrorist groups that were willing to threaten or attack Israel, Jews, Americans, Christians, and even Muslims who oppose Islamic radicalism. The message they spread was that the Jews are possessing ancient Islamic lands and therefore are illegal occupiers. They believe that, without the United States supporting Israel, the newly restored nation will wear down emotionally and economically, and Jews will be forced back into the Gentile nations of the world, thus "liberating" the land for complete Islamic occupation.

THE ROOT PROBLEM

The core issue between much of the Islamic world and Israel is Jerusalem. This ancient city is sacred to three religions: Jews, Christians, and Muslims. Jews consider Jerusalem holy because of Abraham, the prophets, the covenants of God, and so on. Christians pay homage to Jerusalem as the place of redemption through Christ's death, burial, and resurrection. For Muslims, the Jerusalem connection is more complicated.

For Muslims, Jerusalem is linked to the legend of Mohammad's night journey to the furthest mosque, mentioned in Islam's Quran in Surah 17:1. The verse does not mention Jerusalem; it mentions "al-Masjid al-Aqsa" which translates "the furthest mosque." Muslims believe that Mohammad was supernaturally transported at night on a winged creature named Baraq from the black stone at Mecca in Arabia to the furthest mosque, which they say is in Jerusalem. Muhammad is alleged to have ascended to heaven and to have seen heaven, hell, and the famous prophets—all in one night.

While Jerusalem is not mentioned in the story, Muslims began teaching that Jerusalem was the place of the furthest mosque where Mohammad traveled during his alleged night journey. Inside the Islamic Dome of the Rock on the Temple Mount in Jerusalem, visitors are told to place their hand into a wooden case to feel the imprint on the rock of the footprint left by Mohammad's horse when it ascended.

Muhammad died in AD 632 and Muslims took Jerusalem five years later in 637. They built a mosque on the Temple Mount in the late 7th or early 8th century. This means the Temple Mount had no connection to Islam or Muhammad until after Muslims captured the city and built a mosque there years after Muhammad died.

It is believed that, prior to Muslims capturing Jerusalem from the Byzantines in AD 633, there had been a Byzantine Christian structure, possibly a small church or administrative building, at the corner of the Temple Mount close to where the al-Aqsa mosque was later built. The Christian structure was demolished, and around AD 691 the octagonal Dome of the Rock was built as a shrine and prayer center over the rock where Muhammad allegedly ascended to heaven on a horse. Muslims built the al-Aqsa mosque around AD 685-705.

The legend of the night journey to heaven, the capture of Jerusalem, and the construction of the Dome of the Rock and a mosque led Muslims to name Jerusalem their third holiest place. The first is Mecca, Saudi Arabia, the pilgrimage and prayer site where the black cube structure called the Kaaba is located. Medina, Saudia Arabia is the second holiest site because it is the place where Islamic practices developed, as well as the location of Muhammad's elaborate burial site.

Muslims built a mosque and the Dome of the Rock on the site that, in Judaism and Christianity, is the biblical Mount Moriah. This is the site where Abraham was prepared to offer Isaac, and the site of Solomon's Temple, built around 966 BC.

Herein are the facts for the Islamic world. Muslims have complete control over the religion, government, economy, and land in Saudi Arabia, where both Mecca and Media are located. The land mass of just six Islamic countries around Israel—Syria, Iraq, Jordan, Saudia Arabia, Egypt, and Lebanon—is almost a million and a half square miles. The land mass of Israel, *including* the areas in the West Bank that are under full Palestinian Authority control and not Israeli control, is just over ten thousand square miles. If someone is unfamiliar with where Israel is located on a globe, it is almost impossible for them to spot it because it is so tiny.

Muslims control fifteen out of sixteen Middle Eastern countries, which means that Islamic or Islamic-leaning governments control almost ninety-eight percent of the Middle East. In Islamic ideology, especially among the strictest and most devout Muslims, they consider it a grave insult for Christians and especially Jews to live in Jerusalem and throughout Israel. They think the Jews are illegally occupying the land.

In the opinion of many in these nations, including the Shi'ite leadership of Iran, the only way to remove the Jews is by overpowering them in warfare using an Islamic army or an Islamic coalition and deadly missiles and explosives. When people chant, "From the river to the sea, Palestine will be free," they are saying that the Jews should be evicted from this small strip of land between the Jordan River and the Mediterranean Sea. To put this in perspective, the Jordan River is only thirty-five to fifty miles from the Mediterranean, depending on the points measured. These people want the Jews removed from the Middle East entirely, so that Muslims and Islamic governments will control one hundred percent of the Middle East.

Since the Ayatollah's regime took control, Iran's leaders have been strong promoters of antisemitism and Israel hatred in the Middle East. They have used their wealth to fund terrorist militias, military organizations, and countries that will use whatever means possible to kill and destroy the Jews and the state of Israel. According to U.S. and foreign intelligence, the terrorist organizations to which Iran has provided weapons, money, training, and strategies include:

- Hamas, which Iran began to support in the early 1990s. Hamas is an offshoot of the Muslim Brotherhood, and their goal is to destroy Israel as it exists and turn it into an Islamic state.

- Hezbollah, a Shi'ite militant and political group that Iran began to support during the Lebanese Civil War in the 1980s, and whose goal is to eliminate Israel.

- Palestinian Islamic Jihad, a Sunni extremist group that has been primarily funded by Iran since the late 1980s.

Their goal is armed resistance and the establishment of an Islamic Palestinian state.

- Houthi radicals in Yemen, a rebel group that Iran began to support in 2009. Yemen became involved in the war that followed the October 7, 2023 invasion of Israel by shooting missiles into Israel and by attacking commercial ships in the Red Sea and Gulf of Aden.

- Other lesser-known rebel and terrorist groups throughout the Middle East receive support from Iran as well.

The most updated figures indicate that Iran handed over $16 billion dollars to terrorist countries and their terrorist proxies in the eight years between 2012 and 2020. Administrations in the United States had placed various sanctions on Iran for decades due to concerns over issues such as terrorism, nuclear weapons development, and destabilization of the Middle East.

However, in January of 2016, President Obama ordered the delivery of a plane full of cash to Iran in the middle of the night—$400 million to be exact—the same day Iran agreed to release four American prisoners. Another $1.3 billion in interest followed. He alleged this was the settlement of a dispute with Iran that went back to the pre-1979 days of the Shah. In 2021, soon after his inauguration, President Biden unfroze billions of funds to Iran.

I met with members of the Iranian underground church who personally shared with me that, when Iran's Islamic government received the money from the United States, they immediately hired and trained thousands of secret police to identify the leaders in the underground church and persecute or harass them. The same secret police also dealt harshly with any Iranian citizens who expressed a desire for a democratic form of government. They also noted that, years ago when young protesters rose up against the present government, the United States leaders told them that they would stand with the protesters and help them overthrow radical leaders. However, the U.S. never kept their word, and many young people were arrested, tortured, or killed.

THE DAY THAT CHANGED EVERYTHING

The turning point that broke Israel's restraint was the Hamas led October 7, 2023 massacre and kidnappings in southern Israel. In the past when Israeli forces prepared to invade the Gaza Strip and stop the barrage of missiles being fired at them from the area, a sudden cease fire was often called by Hamas to stop Israel's military advancement. Hamas and many of their supporters in the Gaza Strip celebrated the October 7 murder spree, but the reality was that October 7 was the day the Hamas terrorist organization signed their own ticket of destruction.

Intelligence communities in the west knew that Iranian money was supporting the attack. Hamas was the tail of the serpent, but Iran's leadership was the head. Reuters reported that two years before the conflict erupted, Hamas had dug more than 310 miles of tunnels. The Israeli military nicknamed it the Gaza metro. Once the Israeli forces entered the tunnels, they found maps that showed tunnels branching in all different directions. The military discovered an iron-girded tunnel ten feet wide and two-and-a-half miles long that was large enough to drive a car through. This tunnel was near the Erez checkpoint at the Israel – Gaza border. Hamas built other tunnels to cross into Egypt from Gaza so they could secretly bring weapons into Gaza.

A truck that Hamas was using under the guise of bringing food and humanitarian supplies into the Gaza Strip was in fact used to bring ammunition and weapons. Hamas constructed underground facilities beneath hospitals, schools, mosques—places where innocent civilians

The Strongest Middle Eastern Prince Spirit on the Loose

gather—knowing the Israelis would be reluctant to strike those facilities. Hamas terrorists have killed Christians, pastors, their own citizens who stand against them, and communities of innocent people. Medical and military reports, along with photographs and videos of the atrocities in southern Israel, show evil on a level that only demonically possessed people can commit. Hamas even placed a baby in an oven and burned it alive.

Israel knew that eventually, Iran must pay for its decades of attacks conducted both directly and indirectly through proxy militias, as they sought the destruction of the Jewish state. However, Israeli military leaders knew the number of rockets under the control of Hamas and Hezbollah in Lebanon, and they knew that Iran and Syria were replenishing the supply of weapons. If Israel struck Iran, then Hamas and Hezbollah would unleash the gates of hell all at once, overpower Israeli missile defense systems, and cause great destruction throughout Israel.

The prince of Persia united with the radical leaders of the Islamic Republic of Iran after the revolution in 1979. The United States has named Iran the number one sponsor of global terrorism for thirty-nine years in a row. The prince of Persia has been set back for a season, but he continues to work behind the scenes with willing vessels who seek Israel's destruction.

CHAPTER 13

THE PROPHETIC SEVEN-YEAR TREATY

People often ask if the war of Gog of Magog happens before or after the Rapture of the church and the conclusion of the church age known as the "dispensation of the grace of God." Are there clues in the Bible that this war will introduce the seven-year treaty of the Antichrist with Israel? Certain hints within biblical texts give us multiple clues about the timing of these events.

First, the Ezekiel war (chapters 38-39) is not the much-discussed battle of Armageddon (Rev. 16:16). We determine this by comparing the timing of the two battles. The Ezekiel war is fought toward the beginning of the tribulation, while Armageddon occurs at the end of the seven-year tribulation, when Christ returns to earth with the armies of heaven (Rev. 19).

A second clue is that the two battles are not fought at the same locations within Israel. The Ezekiel war occurs on the mountains of Israel, in the far north Golan Heights and east of the Dead Sea. The battle of Armageddon happens when the nations gather in the Valley of Megiddo, which is commonly associated with the Jezreel Valley. The Jezreel Valley is a 145-square-mile plain located in the southern Galilee region, southwest of the Sea of Galilee.

A third indication that these are two separate wars is that Ezekiel mentions five specific nations by name: Persia, Libya, Ethiopia, Gomer, and Togarmah of the north. By comparison, the conflict of Armageddon is led by the kings of the east who are directing two hundred million soldiers (Rev. 9:16). Zechariah presents a clear picture and order of events of this final battle of Armageddon:

> *"For I will gather all nations against Jerusalem to battle; and the city shall be taken, and the houses rifled, and the women ravished; and half of the city shall go forth into captivity, and the residue of the people shall not be cut off from the city. Then shall the Lord go forth, and fight against those nations, as when he fought in the day of battle."*
>
> *And his feet shall stand in that day upon the mount of Olives, which is before Jerusalem on the east, and the mount of Olives shall cleave in the midst thereof toward the east and toward the west, and there shall be a very great valley; and half of the mountain shall remove toward the north, and half of it toward the south."*
>
> – Zechariah 14:2-4 (KJV)

Ezekiel's vision has five nations, while in Zechariah's prophecy, *all nations* are drawn into this conflict. Jerusalem is the focal point. Zechariah notes that:

> *"Behold, I will make Jerusalem a cup of trembling unto all the people round about, when they shall be in the siege both against Judah and against Jerusalem. And in that day will I make Jerusalem a burdensome stone for all people: all that burden themselves with it shall be cut in pieces, though all the people of the earth be gathered together against it."*
>
> – Zechariah 12:2-3 (KJV)

The phrase "cup of trembling" is also used in Isaiah 51:17 and 51:22. In Zechariah, the Hebrew word for cup is *caph*, which refers to a bowl or basin holding blood or wine. The Hebrew word for trembling is *ra'al*, and it conveys the idea of staggering or reeling while intoxicated. We would say they are *drunk for blood* because they are intoxicated with the destruction of the Jewish remnant and Jerusalem.

In Isaiah, the word for cup is *kowc* and the word trembling is *tarelah*, which portrays shock and disorientation at the level of severe discipline and judgment being experienced, and there is no way to avoid it. The cup is forced upon them.

History has shown that the nations and empires that attack Jerusalem eventually find themselves in the ash heap of history. The Egyptian Empire was reduced when God judged Pharaoh with ten plagues, concluding with a death sentence pronounced on all Egyptian firstborn, including the firstborn animals (Exod. 12:12). The Assyrian Empire captured the northern ten tribes that eventually became scattered and known as the Lost Tribes of Israel. The Assyrian Empire faded into history when the Babylonians arose. The Babylonians invaded Judea and Jerusalem, destroyed the Temple, and marched the Jews into bondage in Babylon for seventy years. Eventually, Babylon faded into ruins in the plains of Shinar and became a habitation for animals. The Persian, Greek, and Roman empires all suffered similar fates. They went from ruling the known world of their day to being militarily overtaken by other nations and empires.

JERUSALEM, THE EPICENTER OF CONFLICT

Throughout history, nations and groups have fought over Jerusalem. After the Arabs' successful capture of Jerusalem from the Byzantines, Pope Urban II sent the Crusaders to battle the Muslims and liberate Jerusalem from Muslim dominance in 1099. Between 1096 and 1297, eight crusades were conducted, several of which intended to reach the Holy Land, although not all succeeded.

Many men among the Crusaders believed this war was a holy war. If they participated in the conflict, Catholic Church leaders promised them a path to redemption and a pardoning of all their sins, past, present, and future. In a strange way, this same concept emerged among radicalized Muslims who have a belief that is still held to this day. They believe that if they die in a jihad (holy war) against infidels (non-Muslims, especially Christians and Jews), they are guaranteed entrance into paradise. For making the ultimate sacrifice, as an additional benefit, the members of their family are told that they, too, have a guarantee of a future in paradise.

This explains a reaction to terrorism that people living in most western nations cannot comprehend. In certain areas in the Middle East, when a young man blows himself up as a suicide bomber or when he is killed in a war against the Jews, his mother will often hold up a picture of her son and praise him as a martyr instead of mourning and grieving his death. Her beliefs cause her to reason that his death has now made a clear path for her and the other family members to join him in paradise. In other words, shedding his blood in the service of Allah was doing Allah's work and is pleasing Allah (the Arabic name for God). Jesus warned of this type of ideology;

> "They will put you out of the synagogues; yes, the time is coming that whoever kills you will think that he offers God service. And these things they will do to you because they have not known the Father nor Me."
>
> – JOHN 16:2-4 (NKJV)

Figures about the number of people who died because of the Crusader campaigns are challenging to compile, mostly because of poor medieval recordkeeping. It could have been hundreds of thousands or one to three million. We don't know how many died from the many battles and sieges, or how many died from collateral damage such as famine, disease, and societal disruptions. However, with modern technology and access to data, we do know that, even today, followers of radical Islam conduct regular killing sprees within their own countries. They kill not only Muslims with whom they have sectarian or ethnic differences, they also have wiped out many of the Christians and Jews who didn't flee when they had a chance.

Jews, Christians, and Muslims all claim a strong religious and historical connection to Jerusalem. The Jews will not destroy their most sacred city. True Christians defend Jerusalem, and with the spiritual connection they have to Israel, they will not destroy Jerusalem. The only group remaining to set their focus on Jerusalem are the Islamic nations whose estimated followers number around two billion globally. Most live in the Middle East, northern and central Africa, and parts of Asia. This makes Islam the second-largest religion, with some researchers projecting that by the year 2050, Muslims will outnumber Christians. With an estimated fifteen million Jews and two billion Muslims worldwide, this would be like David fighting 133 giants at one time.

THE SEVEN YEARS CLUE

Biblically, seven is a prominent and significant number. Seven appears hundreds of times in the Bible, beginning with seven days of creation (Gen. 1-2). Seven is identified with completion, finished work, perfection, prophetic completion of time, and is often called "God's perfect number." Seven can also reveal a blessing. However, when dealing with sin, there are times that seven can be associated with God's judgment.

When the Syrian leper Naaman dipped seven times in the Jordan River, his flesh was restored (2 Kings 5:14). Moses wrote that if Israel refused to follow the commandments and chose disobedience and sin instead, the Lord would punish His people seven times more (Lev. 26:18, 24, 28).

There are three seven-year periods that together complete a prophetic puzzle:

- the seven years of Jacob's trouble;
- the seven years when weapons will be burned after the Gog of Magog war;
- the seven years called the Great Tribulation at the end of the age.

Jacob's trouble is a phrase penned in the book of Jeremiah:

> *"Alas! for that day is great, so that none is like it: it is even the time of Jacob's trouble; but he shall be saved out of it."*
>
> – JEREMIAH 30:7 (KJV)

Jacob's trouble began when he took his brother Esau's blessing and birthright. Esau set his eyes upon Jacob to kill him, which caused his mother, out of fear, to send Jacob to her brother Laban's home in Syria. Jacob fell in love and was told by Laban that he must work seven years before marrying his daughter Rachel. At the end of the seven years, Laban intentionally gave Jacob the wrong daughter.

Laban then demanded that Jacob work another seven years to marry Rachel, the love of his life. Laban told Jacob to "fulfill her week" (Gen. 29:27). The Hebrew word for week is *shabua*, which literally refers to a period of seven; in this case, seven years. Jacob labored seven more years to marry the one he didn't get after the first seven years.

The same Hebrew word *shabua* is used in a key end-time prediction in the book of Daniel. This verse is marked as the primary Old Testament passage that introduces the future seven-year tribulation:

> "And he shall confirm the covenant with many for one week: and in the midst of the week he shall cause the sacrifice and the oblation to cease, and for the overspreading of abominations he shall make it desolate, even until the consummation, and that determined shall be poured upon the desolate."
>
> – DANIEL 9:27 (KJV)

This verse reveals the conclusion of a time frame that involved 70 weeks (of years), or 490 years, divided into three distinct time frames. The important time frame for this discussion is the last "week," which is seven years in length. This final week of seven years is decoded in the New Testament to be the seven-year Great Tribulation. In Daniel, a prince that will come (the Antichrist) will confirm a covenant (make a strong agreement) for seven years.

In the middle of the seven years (forty-two months into the agreement), the Antichrist will break the agreement and enter Jerusalem. Here he will set up an abomination, which is the image of the beast that speaks and lives (Rev. 13:11-16), and demand worship of his image. Those who refuse are beheaded:

> "And I saw thrones, and they sat upon them, and judgment was given unto them: and I saw the souls of them that were beheaded for the witness of Jesus, and for the word of God, and which had not worshipped the beast, neither his image, neither had received his mark upon their foreheads, or in their hands;"
>
> – REVELATION 20:4 (KJV)

This final prophetic *week*, or in Hebrew a seven-year time frame, is also revealed in the book of Revelation. The first half is forty-two months, then the firm agreement is broken, thus allowing the Antichrist to rule the last forty-two months.

The dividing moment of the seven years is the breaking of a treaty leading to a war with Egypt, Libya, and Ethiopia, and replacing their leaders with three new ones appointed by the Antichrist (Dan. 7:8). This war campaign is followed by the Antichrist joining with enemies of the Jews, who welcome him to Jerusalem. West Jerusalem and the Jewish quarter of the Old City will be overrun with troops that will raid the dwellings of Jewish people.

There are several reflections in the book of Daniel that mirror the future. One is the metallic image dream of King Nebuchadnezzar (Dan. 2:31-35). A second is King Nebuchadnezzar's seven-year breakdown that forced the king from his throne where he lived outdoors like a beast for seven years. After seven years he was restored to his kingly position (Dan. 4). A third is the fiery furnace that was heated seven times hotter to ensure the deaths of the three young Hebrew men who refused to bow and worship a man-made image (Daniel chapter 3). This reflects the Revelation warning that the Antichrist will make an image and demand worship. Those who refuse will be sentenced to death (Rev. 13:14-15).

SEVEN YEARS TO BURN WEAPONS

Ezekiel contains a significant clue that paints a clearer picture on this prophetic canvas. After the completion of the battle of Gog of Magog, the land where the battle occurred seems to have been polluted in some manner, as men are employed to place markers at every corpse. This search will begin at the end of seven months:

> "At the end of seven months they will make a search. The search party will pass through the land; and when anyone sees a man's bone, he shall set up a marker by it, till the buriers have buried it in the Valley of Hamon Gog."
>
> – Ezekiel 39:14-16 (NKJV)

The Prophetic Seven-Year Treaty

In Jerusalem, when a road is being constructed that requires the removal of trees or buildings, if a bone is found in the ground during the construction process, all work is halted to see if a human bone has been found. The building process could be hindered for months until the area is proven not to be an ancient burial area. If the bone is human, it is respectfully removed and reburied.

After the Gog of Magog war, on the east of the Dead Sea the corpses are buried in mass graves and the area is given a different name, Haman-gog. The most intriguing verse reveals how long it takes to burn the weapons of war used in the conflict:

> *"Behold, it is come, and it is done, saith the Lord God; this is the day whereof I have spoken. And they that dwell in the cities of Israel shall go forth, and shall set on fire and burn the weapons, both the shields and the bucklers, the bows and the arrows, and the handstaves, and the spears, and they shall burn them with fire seven years."*
>
> – Ezekiel 39:8-9 (KJV)

Using primitive weapons from Ezekiel's time, there is no way it would require seven years to burn weapons. In fact, many weapons would be collected by the victors and transferred to their own war arsenal. When the 185,000-man Assyrian army died overnight by a plague sent by God (2 Kings 19:35), the bodies had to be either mass buried, burned with their weapons, or the weapons collected. According to Josephus, when Pharaoh and his six-hundred charioteers drowned in the Red Sea, their weapons washed ashore the following day. The Hebrew men gathered the weapons to use in their future battles

In the Bible, especially English translations, there are words that mean one thing in English but another in the original Hebrew, Aramaic, or Greek languages. Critics point out that the ancient armies burned weapons, especially wooden bows, arrows, wooden structures, catapults, and other primitive military machinery, yet today's modern equipment is made of metals like steel, titanium, and aluminum. Tanks and missiles are not made of wood. Thus, how could Israel "burn" such weapons for seven years? The key is the Hebrew word "burn" used in Ezekiel 39:9.

Several Old Testament Hebrew words are translated into English as "burn." One common word is *saraph*, which means to set something on fire; to burn with fire. The word burn in Ezekiel 39:9 is the word *ba'ra*, which is to kindle to consume something. It can also be translated as "to be brutish; to take something away; cause to eat up, feed, and burn." It could read, "They will take away the weapons with fire." Military forces use many different weapons systems against enemies, and the whole range of weaponry used in an assault is called "fire power." Missiles from land and sea hit targets with fire power that destroys the target and surrounding structures.

Metal weapons that have been blown apart or partially destroyed can be disposed of in a variety of ways. They can be crushed, cut, or melted down and recycled. In Ezekiel 39:9, those living in the cities of Israel will help clear and clean the land in the aftermath. When you see the potential number of troops forming this multitude, you will understand the massive burial and clean up.

Nations Involved	Present Number of Troops	One-Sixth Remain
Libya	76,000 active armed forces	12,666
Ethiopia	362,000 active military personnel	60,333
Persia	610,000 active military personnel	101,666
Turkey	355,000 active military personnel	59,166
Sudan	300,000 active military personnel	50,000

This list shows the active military personnel and not the reservists that each nation can call upon if needed. The total number of active troops currently on this list of nations that will descend upon Israel is 1,703,000, not including others from the north quarters that will join. Based on the present military number, if all troops are involved, over 1.4 million will die in this war.

Israel's surrounding neighbors know that with Israel's technology and intelligence, their air superiority always prevails. These countries understand that they cannot defeat Israel by air assault. The only remaining military strategy is to *overwhelm Israel* from the north, east, and south (the west is the Mediterranean Sea) by outnumbering them in ground forces, fighting face-to-face. They will learn that God's supernatural intervention will once again spare Israel from complete destruction.

During this battle with five Islamic nations and their cohorts, the death rate of five out of six is quite significant. In the past, when the Israeli military decimated an opposing army, often the vanquished enemy signed some type of agreement to avoid a future war. After engaging in wars with Israel, both Egypt and Jordan made peace with Israel.

The Palestinian Liberation Organization leader Yasser Arafat and negotiator Mahmoud Abbas made an agreement with Israeli Prime Minister Yitzhak Rabin in 1993 called the Oslo Accords. In this declaration, Israel agreed to recognize the PLO as the representative of the Palestinians, while the PLO agreed to renounce terrorism and recognize Israel's right to live in peace and security. The Palestinian Authority was established to assume governing responsibilities in the West Bank and Gaza Strip.

This led in 1995 to the West Bank being divided into three separate administrative control areas called Areas A, B, and C, with the goal of ultimately establishing a two-state solution. Israel has responsibility to defend the West Bank from external threats, but beyond that, the control is divided.

The agreement allowed Israel to control Area C, which comprised about sixty percent of the West Bank. Many Jewish people live in this area of the West Bank and the Israeli Defense Forces have military installations there. In Area C, the Palestinian Authority was given control only over civic affairs for the Palestinians who live there.

Area B constitutes twenty-two percent of the West Bank and is heavily populated by Palestinians. Israel controls internal security issues in coordination with the Palestinian Authority, but Israel has no control over public order and civil affairs.

The Palestinian Authority was given complete and exclusive control over Area A, which is eighteen percent of the West Bank. Among the cities under complete Palestinian Authority control are Bethlehem, Jenin, Jericho, Nablus, Qalqilya, Ramallah, Tulkarem, and eighty percent of Hebron. In Area A, the Palestinian Authority is fully responsible for internal security, public order, and civic affairs.

When we take tours to Israel, before our buses enter Bethlehem, each bus must stop at a military checkpoint before we are permitted to enter the city. Here our Jewish guide gets off the bus and does not enter Bethlehem.

The Christian population of Bethlehem steeply declined after the Palestinian Authority took exclusive control. In 1950, Bethlehem was eighty-six percent Christian. In 1994, as one might expect, it was the most populous Christian city in the entire Holy Land. By 2017 the Christian population had dwindled to ten percent. Life has been extremely difficult for Christians living under complete control of the Palestinian Authority.

Prime Minister Yitzhak Rabin was assassinated over his role in the Accords, with many Israelis believing he sacrificed their security. This was followed by a string of terrorist attacks by Hamas. The Oslo

Accords soon collapsed, and as we have seen, the agreement did not achieve the goal of bringing peace and security to Israel.

When the Gog of Magog battle concludes, the Islamic nations will come to some kind of peace agreement with Israel. Daniel 9:27 indicates a treaty will be signed with *many*. This indicates that the agreement is not just with Israel but includes other nations. If the covenant (firm agreement) alluded to in Daniel is the same in Ezekiel, the "many" would include the nations listed— Persia, Libya, Ethiopia, and Turkey, as well as others who were involved in the conflict.

Notice the "seven years" mentioned in both the war of Ezekiel and Daniel's prophecy. Ezekiel notes that seven years are required to burn the invaders' weapons. Daniel then wrote that an agreement would be made with many for seven years (Dan. 9:27). It is possible that the peace treaty of Daniel will include the seven years to destroy the weapons. Thus, there may not be two separate, seven-year agreements.

The Daniel 9:27 treaty and the seven years of burning the weapons could be the same treaty. If this is correct, then the Gog of Magog War is the trigger point for the completion of end-time prophecy.

CHAPTER 14

EZEKIEL'S WAR AND THE RAPTURE LINK

God made it clear to Ezekiel that He would not need human assistance to destroy Israel's invaders. Throughout biblical and secular history, God has used natural disasters to demonstrate His control of nature. In Revelation, John was shown cosmic, land, and sea calamities that will result in the deaths of a third of the global population. The judgments are directed by the Almighty God, who uses angels to release plagues and various other disasters on the earth. Yet every disaster, whether volcanic eruptions, tsunamis, asteroids, solar flares, earthquakes, or floods, can be explained as natural disaster.

Once God has supernaturally intervened to crush and defeat Israel's adversaries on the northern and eastern sides in the Gog of Magog war, the cleanup begins. A unique verse from Ezekiel 39:8 may also be a possible hint: "Behold, it is come, and it is done, saith the Lord God; this is the day whereof I have spoken." The phrase, *it is done*, is also found in Revelation. Notice the context:

> "And he gathered them together into a place called in the Hebrew tongue Armageddon. And the seventh angel poured out his vial

into the air; and there came a great voice out of the temple of heaven, from the throne, saying, It is done."

– REVELATION 16:16-17 (KJV)

"It is done" in Revelation has several possible meanings. In the context of chapter 16, it refers to six angels pouring out six bowl judgments on the earth. When the sixth is poured out the voice says, "It is done" or "It is finished and complete." The setting of this last judgment is toward the end of the tribulation, when the last judgment is released against Mystery Babylon (Rev. 17-18).

In Ezekiel, when God said, "It is done," is He speaking of the Gog of Magog war? When it occurs, does He say, "It is done" to tell the people that what He said over two thousand years ago is now done?

Those who believe in the pre-tribulation Rapture expect the catching away to happen around the time the seven-year agreement is signed—either shortly before, during, or right after. If the seven years of burning weapons are the same seven years of Daniel 9:27, then the possible timing of the Rapture could be connected to the Gog of Magog War.

Since 1948, Israel has been forced to defend its right to exist as a nation, and that always involved fighting Islamic nations that surrounded them. Here are some of the battles they've fought since 1948, and this does not include Palestinian uprisings from within the West Bank.

- 1948-49: War of Independence – Arab countries initiated a war against Israel the day after the state of Israel was officially recognized.

- 1956: Suez Canal Crisis – Israel, Britain, and France attacked Egypt after a crisis with the canal.

- 1967: Six-Day War - Israel launched an air strike against Egypt, Syria, and Jordan after threats of invasion and Syrian attacks from the Golan Heights.

- 1973: Yom Kippur War - Together, Egypt and Syria attacked Israel on the Day of Atonement.

- 1982: Lebanon War - Israel invaded Lebanon to halt deadly attacks from the Palestinian Liberation Organization army.

- 2006: Lebanon War - This conflict between Israel and Hezbollah lasted 34 days.

- 2008-2009: Gaza - Israel voluntarily disengaged from the Gaza Strip and dismantled twenty-one Israeli settlements in 2005, forcing Jews to leave the area. Hamas won the election majority in 2006 and immediately captured Gilad Shalit, an Israeli soldier. In 2008, Israel launched a military offensive in Gaza in response to Hamas rocket attacks on Sderot.

- 2012: Gaza - Israel initiated an offensive attack against Hamas in Gaza due to rocket attacks.

- 2014: Gaza - Hamas kidnapped and killed three Israeli teenagers. Israel launched a military operation against Hamas that lasted seven weeks.

- 2023: October 7th War - Hamas invaded southern Israel where they murdered 1,200 people and kidnapped over 250, including young people who were attending a music festival. This led to a major military operation against

Hamas in the Gaza Strip, where captives were still being held hostage as this book was being written.

- 2024: Israeli-Hezbollah war - Hezbollah joined the Hamas attack against Israel, and in response to the rockets they shot into Israel, an Israeli offensive was launched against Hezbollah in southern Lebanon.

- 2025: Iran Attack - With the knowledge that Iran funded Hamas, Hezbollah, and Houthi terrorists, and following a massive rocket attack against Israel, strikes were launched into Iran to hinder their military and nuclear capabilities.

These wars remind us that there will be "wars and rumors of wars" (Matt. 24:6) and "wars and commotions" (Luke 21:9). The Greek word translated *commotions* refers to instability and disorder, revealing the effects of the wars upon the countries involved. Since the time of ancient Israel, battles have been the triggers to prophetic uprisings, transfers of power, and changes in national governments and the minds of people.

There will come a time of temporary security (peace), but it will be short lived. Paul wrote, "For when they shall say, 'Peace and safety!' then sudden destruction shall come upon them…" (1 Thess. 5:3). In Revelation 6:4, at the time of the four horsemen, we are told that the rider on the red horse is given a great sword and granted power to take peace from the earth. When peace is removed, people start killing each other. The pale horse with a rider named Death, listed as the fourth one that arrives, is given power to kill over one-fourth of the earth's population with sword, famine, pestilence, and wild beasts (Rev. 6:8).

The Antichrist will seize the northern horn of Africa and unite ten nations under his beast coalition. When he arrives in Jerusalem and is hailed for liberating Jerusalem from the Jewish people, the world will ask, "Who can make war with him?" (Rev. 13:4). At this time, he will "make war with the saints and overcome them" (Rev. 13:7). The Greek word used for saints here is *hagios*, which is the common word for saints in the New Testament. The word refers to being pure, blameless, and consecrated. Some suggest this verse is a reference to Christians and the church, thus interpreting it that the Antichrist will make war with and overcome Christians.

First, the "church" is only mentioned in Revelation chapters 2 and 3, and after that the Kingdom of God becomes the theme. Second, by the time the Antichrist seizes Jerusalem, true believers are at the Bema to be judged for their words and actions on earth. This is found in Revelation 11:18: "And the time of the dead, that they should be judged, and that You should reward Your servants the prophets and the saints, and those who fear Your name, small and great."

This is when we receive our rewards. Thus, the true church is in heaven at least by Revelation 11, when the Antichrist kills the two witnesses (Rev. 11:7). This fact indicates that the saints referred to in Revelation 13:4 are a remnant that understands what is happening, has set themselves apart on earth (especially Jews), and are following Christ and rejecting the system of the beast.

John's vision penned in the book of Revelation details one of the greatest assaults of the Antichrist and his ten-nation confederacy. John mentioned a noted city whose religious and political influence impacted the nation. Coded with the name *Mystery Babylon*, most prophetic teachers believe this name conceals the identity of Rome, who was ruling over the earth in John's time. In Europe and the Middle East, people understand that the leading religion that represents Christianity in the west is headquartered in Rome, Italy. More than half of all Catholics live in Africa, Europe, and Asia. (Eastern Orthodox

Christians split from the Catholic Church in 1054 and are not under the authority of the Vatican or the Catholic Church.) The Vatican in Rome is a state unto itself.

Most Muslims view the Vatican and Rome as the global headquarters for Christianity. Revelation chapters 17 and 18 mention Mystery Babylon. Whatever this mysterious religious and political center is, John saw it being destroyed in one hour (see Rev. 18).

Revelation 13:11 speaks of another beast coming out of the earth that had "two horns like a lamb, but he spoke like a dragon." Of the twenty-seven times that the word *lamb* is used in the book of Revelation, twenty-six of the references symbolize the lamb as Christ. But in Revelation 13:11, this lamb is the False Prophet. He is coming as a false Christian leader, and the two horns represent his uniting of two religions under his influence—apostate Christianity and Islam.

If, as most believe, this False Prophet is an apostate pope who will be joining these two religions, then he cannot sit on the traditional Pope's seat at the Vatican. Islam would never allow this. Jerusalem is the perfect location, however, as it is accepted as sacred by both Muslims and Christians.

The Antichrist will build a new political-military complex by uniting the ten nations, while the False Prophet will unite two religions to create a new religion. He will perform false signs and wonders, such as making fire come down from heaven onto earth, and people will see it with their own eyes. He will create an image of the beast and be given the power to make the image live and speak. The False Prophet will demand worship of this image, and those who refuse to do so will be killed (Rev. 13:11-16).

In Revelation 17:12–13, the ten nations give their kingdoms to the Antichrist in the timeframe of one hour. Why would they do this? The answer is simple: for the survival of their own nations. All buying and selling will be controlled through the mark of the beast. The Antichrist will have the ability to control food supplies. He will use weapons of mass destruction against resistant nations. Out of fear, some world leaders will capitulate and give their nations to the Antichrist, who will have the ability to utterly destroy them. How do I know this? Here is what Daniel wrote about the Antichrist:

> "But rumors from the east and from the north shall alarm and hasten him. And he shall go forth with great fury to destroy and utterly to sweep away many."
>
> – Daniel 11:44 (AMP)

The Antichrist will behead those who refuse to follow him (Rev. 20:4). Why would he do this? What benefit is there for him and his ten-nation beast system to slaughter so many people? I believe one answer is found in the book of Revelation.

When the asteroid called wormwood strikes, a third of the fresh drinking water is poisoned, causing death (Rev. 8:11). The famines are too widespread, and people are dying by the millions from famine. During the first forty-two months of the seven-year tribulation, it does not rain in the area where the beast system is operating (Rev. 11:6). This alone will cause severe food shortages and rationing.

This could provide a hint for why people are beheaded. The fewer mouths to feed, the more food and water available for the Antichrist and his coalition. The puzzle is complete when we understand that no man can buy or sell without the mark, the name, or the number of the beast (Rev. 13:17). It also cannot be denied that some sects of Islam accept beheading of unbelievers, as stated in the Quran in sura 8:12-13 and 47:4. Western audiences have been horrified to witness this in our own lifetimes, especially during the Second Gulf War with Iraq.

According to John's vision in Revelation 13, the False Prophet will become the right-hand man for the Antichrist. It will appear to many that the only way to survive is to sell their souls to the religious system of the False Prophet. Throughout history, people have forsaken their religion for another, just to ensure their survival. They have sold all they had or even betrayed family for short term relief. Billions of people will perish during the seven-year tribulation period that is coming in the future. The hope for the believer is in the return of Christ and the resurrection of the dead in Christ.

CHAPTER 15

WHEN A DEAD HEAD RISES AGAIN

Some time back, the History Channel decided to produce a documentary about Bible prophecy in which they interviewed various ministers who taught the subject. I was asked for an interview. The television crew came to my ministry studio, set up cameras, lights, and microphones, and two chairs facing each other. One was for the gentleman asking me questions.

After discussing the Antichrist, the gentleman asked me, "Do you believe that, when the Antichrist receives a deadly head wound, his wound will be healed and he will be resurrected as a mockery of Christ?"

I replied, "Actually, that's not what the scripture teaches." The host turned to the film crew and told them to stop the cameras. I turned the Bible to Revelation 13 and read the text: "And I saw one of his heads as if it had been mortally wounded, and his deadly wound was healed. And all the world marveled and followed the beast."

I said, "How many heads does one human have? Just one. The Antichrist is a human man with one head. John said that one of his heads was mortally wounded. The heads referred to are the seven heads of the dragon, which are the seven empires of prophecy" (Rev. 13:1-3). I listed the nations of Egypt, Assyria, Babylon, Medo-Persia, Greece,

Rome, and the seventh being the coalition that rules during the first part of the tribulation.

It is one of these heads that receives a death wound, but the dead head rises again. It is a region of the world, a past empire that does not currently exist. It is the reunification of the ancient Babylonian empire, as Babylonia is the only head in the group that doesn't exist today. This head is a reunification of old empires.

> *"Now the beast which I saw was like a leopard, his feet were like the feet of a bear, and his mouth like the mouth of a lion. The dragon gave him his power, his throne, and great authority."*
>
> – REVELATION 13:2 (NKJV)

The symbolism used in Daniel to describe three of the four beasts coming out of the earth are a leopard, a bear, and a lion. Historically, those symbols represent empires:

- the lion - a symbol of the Babylonian Empire
- the bear - a symbol of the Medo-Persian Empire
- the leopard - a symbol of the Grecian Empire.

When we combine the lands that were historically under the control of those three empires, the territory covers the following modern nations:

- Greece
- Lebanon
- Assyria (Syria)
- Iraq
- Iran
- Israel

- Jordan (specifically, Edom, Moab, and Ammon)
- Turkey
- Egypt
- Afghanistan
- Pakistan

Islam is the primary religion in nine of the eleven nations listed. Most of these Islamic nations have a small population of Christians, some of whom are forced to worship in secret. The forced secrecy makes it difficult to determine the country's actual numbers of Christians.

Greece is predominantly Greek Orthodox, and Israel is predominantly Jewish, followed by Muslim, then followed by Christian and a few other religions.

Pakistan has a growing Christian community, especially in the villages. This is one country where the raw number of Christians is rising.

Coptic Orthodox Christians represent ninety percent of Christians in Egypt. The total Christian population there is said to be around ten million, which represents about ten percent of the population. The Egyptian government recognizes other religions, but radicals have attacked many churches in the last decade and persecuted Christians.

Lebanon has had a Christian presence since the first century. In the 1980s, Christians represented as high as fifty-five percent of the population, but war, political instability, Christian migration, and Muslim immigration reduced those numbers. The Christian population now shows as low as thirty percent, with most reports using the estimate of around 2.24 million Christians in Lebanon. This once predominately Christian country is now predominately Muslim.

With Turkey's total population of around eighty-five million people, the Christian population there is estimated to be less than half of one percent of the total population. Turkey had a strong Christian community at one time, between three and four million in the mid-nineteenth century. By 1924, genocide, forced conversions, abductions, and deportations significantly reduced the Christian population.

Tradition says that Christianity was brought to Iraq in the first century by the Apostle Thomas. At the beginning of the 21st century, there were 1.5 million Christians in Iraq, but today the Christian population is said to be around 140,000, less than one percent of the population. When the Islamic State took over Mosul in 2014, many Christians fled the country and have not returned because of Islamic hostility toward them.

Syria also has a Christian community that dates back to the first century AD. The road to Damascus was where Saul, who later became the Apostle Paul, experienced his conversion. Before Syria's 2011 civil war, the Christian population was estimated to be as high as two million. Today the number has dropped to an estimated 300,000. Churches were destroyed during the civil war. Islamic persecution has helped destroy the Christian population in Syria, and terrorist groups affiliated with the new leader of Syria, who was installed in a 2025 coup against Assad, have slaughtered a thousand Christians.

Afghanistan's Christian history goes back to the second century. There is no way to currently know for sure how many Christians are in the country because they are underground and do not identify themselves. Conversion from Islam is punishable by death. There could be as few as two thousand Christians or as many as ten thousand Christians in Afghanistan. Open Doors World Watch ranks Afghanistan as the second worst country for Christians, behind North Korea.

Iran is one country that has experienced astonishing growth of its underground church, especially among the young people. In 2022, Open Doors International estimated there are 1.24 million believers in Iran. Those numbers are likely to be even higher today.

These are countries that fall within the missionary definition of the 10/40 window. Geographically, this is the section of the globe that is positioned between ten degrees north and forty degrees north latitude and includes most of the world's Muslim, Buddhist, and Hindu religious adherents. Forty-two percent of the world's population lives within the 10/40 window.

Clearly, the total Christian population of the Middle East is small and has dropped significantly over the years, while the Muslim population has dramatically increased. I once asked a high-ranking individual with a federal agency to give me our government's estimate of the number of radicalized Muslims. At that time, she suggested at least two hundred million and possibly more. My mind went to John's vision of a 200-million-man army that will march across the Euphrates River which, oddly, has been slowly drying up (Rev. 16:12).

Iraq is the same land where the ancient city of Babylon was located, which was the center of the Babylonian Empire in the 18th century BC, and again in the 7th century BC under Nebuchadnezzar. Iraq, which borders Iran, is divided unequally between Sunni and Shi'ite Muslims.

In Iran, Shi'ite Muslims are the largest religious group, with ninety-three percent of the population claiming to follow that branch of Islam. Shi'ite Islam has been the official religion of Iran since the early 16th century.

Where does most of the fighting occur in the Middle East? The nations that continually make the news cycle and house or assist the most terrorists are Southern Lebanon, Syria, Iraq, and Iran. The early Babylonian Empire was centered in Iraq, Syria, Lebanon, part of Turkey, and part of Iran. The Babylonians also laid siege to Jerusalem and Judea. The areas listed above are believed by many to be the headquarters of the Antichrist for the first forty-two months. The second forty-two months, he will set himself in Jerusalem.

> "And he shall pitch his palatial tents between the seas and the glorious holy mountain [Zion]. Yet he shall come to his end, with none to help him."
>
> – Daniel 11:45 (ESV)

Between the seas refers to the land between the Dead Sea (referred to as the Salt Sea in the Old Testament) and the Mediterranean Sea. Jerusalem, called the glorious holy mountain in this passage, is positioned on a series of hills in the Judean Mountains between these two bodies of water.

According to scripture, there will eventually be a Jewish Temple constructed on the Temple Mount in Jerusalem. Of course, Muslims adamantly oppose this idea because they consider the Temple Mount their possession and have marked it as such with the Al Aqsa mosque and the large, octagonal-shaped Dome of the Rock. When the two witnesses show up at the beginning of the tribulation, they will have authority to close the heavens and call fire down up men. Several early church fathers believed these two men were Elijah and Enoch, both of whom were transported to heaven without experiencing death. They will return to Jerusalem to preach and to spiritually secure the 144,000 Jewish men through a seal of God that protects them from danger (Rev. 7).

According to my Jewish sources, including some who served in the Hebrew University, due to the number of rituals required and the laws of the ancient Temple, the new facility would not be ready for worship for about three and one-half years. This is the length of time the two witnesses will minister before both are killed when the Antichrist invades Jerusalem (Rev. 11:7). It could possibly be the dedication of the Temple that will move the armies of this man of sin toward the Holy City. Daniel wrote that he will set up an abomination on the wing of the Temple:

> *"...So he shall return and show regard for those who forsake the holy covenant. And forces shall be mustered by him, and they shall defile the sanctuary fortress; then they shall take away the daily sacrifices, and place there the abomination of desolation."*
>
> – Daniel 11:30-31 (NKJV)

The abomination of desolation is mentioned by Christ in Matthew 24:15:

> *"Therefore when you see the 'abomination of desolation,' spoken of by Daniel the prophet, standing in the holy place" (whoever reads, let him understand), then let those who are in Judea flee to the mountains. Let him who is on the housetop not go down to take anything out of his house. And let him who is in the field not go back to get his clothes."*
>
> – Matthew 24:15-18 (NKJV)

In scripture, idol worship is considered an abomination (Ezek. 18:12). After the Antichrist seizes Jerusalem, including the Temple Mount, one of his first acts is to set up an image (icon in Greek) which will speak and live, and demand that all people worship the image or face death. This is why many Jews will flee from Jerusalem and head into the wilderness of Moab, as the country of Jordan (called Edom, Moab, and Amman) is the only nation that will escape the control of the Antichrist (see Daniel 11:41).

The Antichrist becomes the hero of the Islamic nations that have been waiting for someone to "liberate" Jerusalem from Jewish political, economic, and spiritual control. Once he enters the glorious land, this will begin the final forty-two months of the Great Tribulation.

CHAPTER 16

THE CONFUSION OVER WHO IS GOG OF MAGOG

The name Gog is mentioned in both the Old and New Testaments. Gog is first mentioned in 1 Chronicles 5:4 in the genealogy of a man named Joel: "The sons of Joel; Shemaiah his son, Gog his son...." The other nine Old Testament references are mentioned in Ezekiel 38 and 39.

The etymology of the name Gog is uncertain. However, there is a Hebrew verb *gud* which conveys the idea of raiding, assembling to attack, and ambushing. In some Slavic countries, Gog is a surname that is passed down generationally.

What is the confusion over the name Gog? Ezekiel identifies Gog as the chief prince of Meshech and Tubal. Gog is a spirit, but Gog is also a man who directs or supports Meschech and Tubal (Ezek. 38:2-3, 39:1). These are biblical names that perhaps can be identified through ancient history.

Early teachers of Bible prophecy considered Meschech and Tubal to be Russia, and they taught that this war would be a Russian invasion. It is true that the former Soviet Union (USSR) provided military aid to many countries around the world, including Egypt, Syria, Iraq, and parts of Africa. They provided significant military support to Egypt and Syria during their wars against Israel in 1967 and 1973. Since the fall of the Soviet Union in 1991, Russia has also supported Syria and Iran militarily. However, Meshech and Tubal might not be modern Russia, but another nation that is closer to Israel than Russia.

THE TABLE OF NATIONS

Moses and the Prophets did an outstanding job recording the fathers and their descendants who formed the early nations. The list of nations is found in Genesis 10 and 1 Chronicles 5. The Genesis record names the three sons of Noah—Shem, Ham, and Japeth—as well as their sons and their sons' sons who scattered throughout the Middle East, Northern Africa, and Asia. Ham's family is linked with Northern Africa, Shem with the Middle East, and Japeth with Asian countries. The scripture reads:

> *"Now these are the generations of the sons of Noah, Shem, Ham, and Japheth: and unto them were sons born after the flood. The sons of Japheth; Gomer, and Magog, and Madai, and Javan, and Tubal, and Meshech, and Tiras. And the sons of Gomer; Ashkenaz, and Riphath, and Togarmah."*
>
> *– Genesis 10:1-3 (KJV)*

Notice that the sons of Japeth are the names of those involved in the future war of Gog of Magog, as they are also listed in Ezekiel 38:2-6. They are Magog, Meshech, Tubal, Gomer, and Togarmah (a grandson). These men were all descendants of Noah. The earliest names of the descendants of Meshech and Tubal place their people in central Anatolia, which is modern Turkey. According to Assyrian records, Meshech (called Mushki in the records) and Tubal (called Tabali in the records) were known for copper trading and metal working, and for trading captured people—slave trade.

Some early ministers of Bible prophecy taught that Meshech was Moscow and Tubal was Tobolsk in Russia. This idea was based on the phonetic similarity of the names, but it lacks historical evidence. It would be like taking the word "chief" in Ezekiel 38:2, which is the Hebrew word *ro'sh*, meaning head, top, or beginning (such as head or beginning of the year) and saying this is Russia. People sometimes take a word and attempt to make it mean something it does not, simply based on the phonetic sound of the word. One man taught that Jesus means "praise Zeus" because the last three letters of the English name for Jesus is "sus." Not only is that incorrect, but it's also preposterous.

According to scholars who study the history of ancient lands, Meshech and Tubal are associated with Asia Minor, or more specifically, modern day Turkey. Once called Anatolia, Turkey has played a major role in both ancient and modern history. It is the location of the seven churches that Christ addressed in Revelation chapters 2 and 3. Ephesus, Smyrna, Pergamum, Thyatira, Sardis, Philadelphia, and Laodicea were all located in modern Turkey. Today tourists visit these destinations to view historic ruins and hear guides discuss their ancient history. Turkey is biblically and historically part of ancient and future prophecy. They have the capability to lead a future coalition against Israel.

In the Ezekiel 38 - 39 Gog of Magog War, one of the nations that attacks Israel from the north is Togarmah. Scholars debate over the location of modern Togarmah, with the majority accepting the theory that ancient Togarmah was the region of Armenia and Turkey. The Jewish historian Josephus confirms this because he linked Togarmah with the Phrygians who lived in Asia Minor. They likely migrated to Anatolia in the 2nd millennium, after the collapse of the Hittite Empire. Ezekiel noted that Togarmah is from the "north quarters," and they will organize others to join with them in the battle.

This is a sensible conclusion when we consider the Ottoman Empire that formed in 1299 and ended in 1922, followed by the establishment of the Republic of Turkey in 1923. At the empire's peak in the sixteenth century, they ruled over or had some level of control over countries in Southeastern Europe, including Bulgaria, Albania, Serbia, Montenegro, Kosovo, Greece, North Macedonia, Bosnia and Herzegovina, and parts of Romania, Hungary, Slovenia, Croatia, and Ukraine. Their territories included parts of Africa—Algeria, northern Sudan, northern Chad, Egypt, Libya, and Tunisia. They controlled all of modern Turkey, Iraq, Syria, Israel (known then as Palestine), Jordan, Lebanon, Qatar, parts of Saudi Arabia, Armenia, Iran, Georgia, Oman, and Azerbaijan. Significant portions of Europe, Africa, and Asia were under Ottoman control. It was an expansive and grand empire at one time.

From 1291 to 1517, the Mamluk Sultanate of Egypt controlled the city of Jerusalem, but he was defeated by the Ottomans. This gave the Ottomans access to Jerusalem. Gradually, the empire began to wane, with westerners calling it the "sick man of Europe." After World War I, the declining Ottoman Empire collapsed and was carved into several pieces. Control of Iraq, Transjordan, and Israel (Palestine), at least for a time, fell under the British Mandate. Israel achieved independence as its own state in 1948.

From 1915 to 1917, the Ottomans killed Armenian Christians in Anatolia (Turkey), starting in Constantinople. Armenian Christians made up a significant portion of inhabitants—two and a half million of them—and they shared the area with Muslim Kurds. The Armenian Christians were treated harshly by the Kurds, and the courts always seemed to favor the Muslims. As the Ottoman Empire began to struggle and suffer various military defeats, the Young Turks shifted blame to the Armenians. By the time the war ended, ninety percent of the Armenian Christians had either been deported or massacred. An estimated million to million and a half Armenia Christians were killed, while women and children who survived were forced to convert to Islam.

Today, Turkey is ranked in the top ten of global military powers, and they have one of the strongest armies in the Middle East. It has been a dream among some Muslims to reunite all the lands that were lost at the fall of the Ottoman Empire and put them all under the Islamic banner. If they were to succeed, they would essentially forge a new Turkish Empire.

THE BOOK OF THE WAR OF THE LORDS

One perplexing verse is Ezekiel 38:17, where Ezekiel wrote about Gog and stated:

> "Thus says the Lord God: "Are you he of whom I have spoken in former days by My servants the prophets of Israel, who prophesied for years in those days that I would bring you against them?"
>
> – Ezekiel 38:17 (NKJV)

From creation in Genesis 1 to the prophecy of Ezekiel 38, about 3,400 years passed. The war of Gog is only mentioned one time in biblical writings, and that was by Ezekiel. Yet Ezekiel wrote that God spoke to the prophets of Israel in the past about Gog, who prophesied for years that a war was coming. Was this written down somewhere else before Ezekiel wrote about it? Why is the book of Ezekiel the first time we hear about this war?

The Bible mentions four books that are not part of the canon of scripture and are considered lost. They are:

1. the Book of Jasher, mentioned in Joshua 10:13 and 2 Samuel 1:18

2. the Book of Nathan the Prophet, mentioned in 1 Chronicles 29:29

3. the Book of Gad the seer, mentioned in 1 Chronicles 29:29

4. the Book of the Wars of the LORD, mentioned in Numbers 21:14.

These books were known and read in ancient times but were lost over many centuries. There is currently a Book of Jasher, but there are several versions of it, so it cannot be taken as one hundred percent factual. Nobody can be certain what was written by the prophets about wars. However, it is clear from Ezekiel that certain prophets before Ezekiel saw this battle coming, and they had prophesied that God would bring Gog down against Israel.

While this is an assumption, it is certainly possible that one or more of these lost books contain information about this war that Ezekiel refers to. Perhaps some of the information Ezekiel wrote was known in his day, and he simply added the prophetic insight that God revealed to him as he detailed this end-time war with enemy nations coming against Israel.

THE CONTROVERSY OF GOG

There is also strong discussion over a reference to Gog in Revelation chapter 20:

> *"Now when the thousand years have expired, Satan will be released from his prison and will go out to deceive the nations which are in the four corners of the earth, Gog and Magog, to gather them together to battle, whose number is as the sand of the sea. They went up on the breadth of the earth and surrounded*

the camp of the saints and the beloved city. And fire came down from God out of heaven and devoured them"

– REVELATION 20:7-9 (NKJV)

It is generally accepted that Gog is the name of a man who will organize the armies against Israel. Yet, at the end of Christ's one-thousand-year reign, the name Gog reappears as he joins with Satan to inspire the nations to come against the camp of the saints (Jerusalem) for one final conflict. As this massive army surrounds Jerusalem, God will send fire to devour them. He then removes Satan from the earth to join the Antichrist and False Prophet in the lake of fire. If Gog is a name, why does he continue to be present on earth from Ezekiel 38, past the thousand-year reign of Christ? An answer to this question is concealed in the Ezekiel text.

Three times in Ezekiel 38 and 39, Gog is called *the chief prince*. The Hebrew word for chief (KJV) is *ro'sh*, which is the word for "head," and it can also refer to a high-ranking leader. I heard many prophetic ministers in the 1980s say that *ro'sh* was Russia. But as I mentioned earlier, in Hebrew and from historical references, *ro'sh*, or chief, simply means head.

Then there is the word *prince*, used ninety-two times throughout the Old Testament. The word "prince" is used for both an earthly ruler and angels in both the Kingdom of God and the kingdom of Satan. Jacob (Gen. 32:28), the leaders of the tribes of Israel (Num. 34:18,) and David (Ezek. 37:25) are all called a prince. The common Hebrew word used for prince is *nasi'* which is translated as "captain, prince, governor, ruler." A prince is someone with a high ruling position who is given authority and control over kingdoms, nations, and empires.

In Daniel 10:21, Michael the archangel is called "your prince." In Daniel 12:1, Michael is called "the great prince who stands watch over the children of your people." These facts present us with another possibility for Gog's identity.

First, Gog is some type of military leader and organizer who unites nations against Israel and against the saints. Gog is also given authority over a specific area of the earth—Magog, Meshech, and Tubal. God declares to Gog, "I am against you" (Ezek. 35:3; 39:1). At the end of the war, Ezekiel noted, "I will give Gog a burial place there in Israel," and "there they will bury Gog and all his multitudes" (Ezck. 39:11). Over a thousand years from now, when Satan is once against loosed for a short time, Gog reappears. How is this possible?

GOG - A MAN AND A PRINCE DEMON

In Daniel, Michael the archangel is called a prince—the Hebrew word being *sar*, which refers to a chief ruler of various spheres. The same word was used in Daniel 10:13 and 20 when Daniel wrote of two opposing spirits—the prince of Persia and the prince of Greece—that were working to hinder both him and Israel by blocking the understanding of prophecy. These were two high ranking agents within the kingdom of Satan, whose goal was to position themselves in certain nations and watch the movement of leaders, both military and religious, and to hinder or thwart the plans of God by whatever means necessary.

When Satan offered Jesus the kingdoms of the world (which would have been through the Roman Empire) if only Jesus would bow His knees and worship him, Satan revealed:

> *"Then the devil, taking Him up on a high mountain, showed Him all the kingdoms of the world in a moment of time. And the devil said to Him, "All this authority I will give You, and their glory; for this has been delivered to me, and I give it to whomever I wish. Therefore, if You will worship before me, all will be Yours."*
>
> *– Luke 4:5-7 (NKJV)*

The Confusion Over Who Is Gog of Magog

The decision over who will rule individual nations is sometimes determined by voting, or in some places a dictator remains in authority until he is forcefully removed, killed, goes into exile, or dies. With voting, there is the will of the people and the will of God. The Lord planned for Israel to quickly retake the Promised Land. However, after the negative report from ten spies, the Hebrew people voted and refused to enter because of fear and unbelief. Sometimes God gives people what they voted for; and like the Israelites, they must wander in the desert because of their decision.

All nations in the world have spiritual powers of angels and demonic rulers that battle over the will of God, fulfillment of prophecy, and power and position in those nations. This includes countries like China, Russia, Turkey and other key nations involved in end-time prophecy.

So, who or what is Gog?

- Gog was first mentioned in the Bible as a man born to a human.

- Gog was known among the earthly prophets as someone leading a great war against Israel.

- Gog in both testaments is connected to Turkey, Armenia, and parts of Russia.

- Gog and his armies will be destroyed in the Gog of Magog war in the future.

- Gog reappears to assist Satan in the war against Jerusalem at the end of the 1,000-year reign.

This tells us that Gog is a person, a ruler of the north country, and likely the name of a chief satanic principality that influences certain nations—politically, religiously, and militarily.

Clay cuneiform tablets are some of the earliest forms of written communication and were used before an alphabet system was created. On early tablets, the Scythians were called "Ga-agi," which may be a linguistic link to the name Gog. The Sumerians, one of the earliest civilizations in the Fertile Crescent, were located in Mesopotamia, which had at its core the land of Iraq. The Sumerians used a word "kukkug" to describe darkness.

After researching the name and meaning of Gog from various sources, my conclusion is that Gog carries three possible meanings:

- Gog can be the name of a military and political commander who oversees the northern armies.

- Gog is linked with a region of the world where darkness rules (Turkey and perhaps parts of the former Ottoman Empire).

- Gog can be the name of the principality that rules north of Israel and among Israel's enemies.

Every angel of God was given a name. Every spirit in the kingdom of darkness also has a name. In the New Testament there are foul spirits, unclean spirits, evil spirits, spirits of infirmity, deaf and dumb spirits, seducing spirits, and so forth. The evil spirit takes on the nature of the sin or sickness it is associated with. In 2 Chronicles 18:18, there is a "lying spirit" that motivated Ahab's prophets to lie. Other names identify their area of rule.

In a strange vision, Zechariah saw four chariots coming out from between two large mountains of brass. The horses with the chariots had colors: red, black, white, and dappled. These are the four angelic spirits assigned to go out to the north, the south, and to and fro throughout the earth (Zech. 6:1-7).

Likewise, there are demonic spirits that are assigned over these parts of the earth. I believe that one of those spirits is named Gog. Many men have the name Michael, and at the same time, that is the name of God's chief angel. My son's middle name is Gabriel. He was born near Christmas, and I named him after the angel Gabriel.

Gog could be the name of a spirit that will return from the abyss at the end of the thousand-year reign of Christ. At the same time, Gog can also be the name of a human who will oversee the war that is coming.

CHAPTER 17

THIS WILL SHOCK THE WORLD

Egypt and Jordan were considered enemies of modern Israel in 1948, and at times they combined their military forces with Syria to attack Israel from the north, south, and east. After the Six-Day War in 1967 and Syria's defeat in the 1973 Yom Kippur War, Syria began to back away from attacking Israel. They still held claim to the Golan Heights, even after Israel formally annexed it. Instead of a peace agreement, the United Nations established a buffer zone between the two countries.

In March of 1979, the Israel-Egypt Peace Treaty was signed, which normalized relations and settled disputes between the two countries. Egypt became the first Arab country to officially recognize Israel and make peace.

Then in October of 1994, Israel signed a peace agreement with Jordan which settled territorial disputes and normalized relations. On any given day, trucks go back and forth between Israel and Jordan as the two countries trade vegetables, grains, fruits, and supplies. As part of the agreements with Egypt and Jordan, organized cross border tourism is allowed.

There are seven Persian Gulf nations known as the Gulf Arab States: Iraq, Kuwait, Saudi Arabia, Bahrain, Qatar, United Arab Emirates, and Oman. All are Islamic, but some have more religious tolerance than others. Most are oil producers to some degree, with the Gulf States bringing in hundreds of billions of dollars a year from oil exports. They all recognize the need for economic diversification. Iran is also situated on the Persian Gulf, but that is not considered an Arab nation.

For decades, many of the Gulf States have enjoyed doing business with America. They collected our oil dollars and invested in our stock market and institutions. However, their relationships with Israel have ranged from a muted, working relationship to hostility. Political tensions and the ongoing Palestinian conflict are blamed for this, although religious differences and ideology certainly play a role as well.

THE ABRAHAM ACCORDS

The common link between Jews, Muslims, and Christians is Abraham. He is the natural father of the Jews through Isaac and the natural father of the Arabs through Ishmael. Abraham is important to Christians because Christ's lineage is also through Abraham, Isaac, and Jacob.

During President Trump's first term, he brokered an agreement called the Abraham Accords, which were intended to promote diplomatic relations, economic cooperation, and security between Israel and any Arab nations that signed the accords. The initial agreement was signed by Bahrain, the United Arab Emirates, Morocco, and Sudan. The Abraham Accords would provide opportunities for trade and commerce, defense and security, and closer relations in general.

The one country that has indirectly hindered others from joining this agreement is Iran. Since 1984 Iran has been labeled a state sponsor of terrorism. Under the Ayatollah's regime, the Iranian government has funded and trained militant terrorist groups throughout the Middle East, including Hamas in Gaza, Hezbollah in Lebanon, and Palestinian groups in the West Bank. Their fingerprints are found in Syria, Iraq, and Yemen. The goal is to form an anti-Semitic and anti-Israel resistance, using missiles, drones, and whatever means necessary to attack Israel and innocent people. Let's be aware that these terrorist groups do not attack only Israel; they destroy anybody who stands against them, including citizens in their own countries. The conflict between Sunni and Shi'ite Muslims goes back 1,400 years and still exists to this day.

THE FIVE LETTER WORD IS OUT

Immediately after the U.S. bombed three underground nuclear research and uranium enrichment facilities in Iran in 2025, the news was flooded with one five-letter word: peace. President Trump immediately called on Iran's leaders to come to the table and make peace. On a Sunday afternoon, every network was parroting the phrase, "We need peace," and "Now is the time to move toward peace and security." Some were certain this attack on the nuclear facilities in Iran would lead to peace for Israel and the Middle East, while others were telling us this would lead to World War III.

War-weary people are calling for a stop to all wars and conflicts. Whether it is Russia and Ukraine, India and Pakistan, China and Taiwan, or war throughout the Middle East, people are calling for peace. Generally speaking, the public and especially some of the younger people don't understand why countries cannot simply make peace with other nations.

The first letter Paul wrote in the New Testament was First Thessalonians. In 1 Thessalonians 4:16-17, he penned a revelation he received on Mount Sinai in Arabia (Gal. 1:17; 4:25). Paul wrote of the catching away of the living and the resurrection of the dead in Christ, when Christ returns for those who have served Him. In chapter five, Paul connects the catching away of believers (an event referred to as the Rapture) to something very important. These things are not always linked together in the minds of believers, but they should be.

> "But concerning the times and the seasons, brethren, you have no need that I should write to you. For you yourselves know

perfectly that the day of the Lord so comes as a thief in the night. For when they say, "Peace and safety!" then sudden destruction comes upon them, as labor pains upon a pregnant woman. And they shall not escape."

– 1 Thessalonians 5:1-3 (NKJV)

The Greek word for safety is *asphaleia*, which can literally or figuratively mean security, as in security from enemies and danger. People will exclaim with joy that the world has arrived at a time of "peace and security." Just when things seem peaceful and nations are settling into a sense of false security, then sudden destruction comes, and they cannot escape! The word destruction in Greek carries the idea of utter destruction and the death that comes with it, although it does not imply total annihilation.

With fears of rouge nations obtaining nuclear weapons and being crazed enough to use them, we can see how modern weapons will potentially cause that kind of death and destruction. Even severe natural disasters can result in a lack of peace and safety, as people who have lost everything and have no food are in chaos, with some fighting over whatever they can find.

Paul mentioned the coming of the Lord in all five chapters of First Thessalonians. In this setting, the Spirit of God inspired him to speak of a time when people will be clamoring for and believing they finally have peace and safety.

Some suggest that the season of peace and security will be forced upon Israel and the surrounding Islamic nations following the outcome of the Gog of Magog War. The defeated nations will demand some type of military ceasefire and possible disarmament. Daniel 9:27 identifies the seven-year treaty that will be signed, and it gives the first foreshadowing of the seven-year tribulation when a covenant (agreement) is made with *many*, referring to many nations.

CHAPTER 18

GOD'S FOUR WEAPONS OF DESTRUCTION ARE COMING

In the book of Revelation, when the trumpet and bowl judgments are released, John observed angels blowing trumpets and tipping the bowls. Each blast and bowl being poured out unleashes a specific judgment upon the earth. Many tribulation judgments are either cosmic events or natural disasters that happen suddenly and cause significant damage to property and death to humans and animals.

Look at the second trumpet judgment. Something like a great mountain burning with fire is cast into the sea, and a third of the sea becomes blood, a third of the sea creatures die, and a third of the ships are destroyed (Rev. 8:8-9). This can be understood as a massive volcanic eruption that impacts a significant portion of life on earth. This volcanic eruption would almost certainly result in an earthquake and then a tsunami that will destroy an entire one-third of all human life, sea life, and ships.

During the 2004 Indian Ocean tsunami that was caused by an underground earthquake, locations all around the ocean were affected. It is still considered the worst natural disaster in history, as nearly 228,000 people were killed and fifteen countries were affected. Cargo ships, fishing boats, and barges were destroyed. A 2,600-ton ocean vessel was carried over a mile inland where it still remains. A Thai naval boat was flung over a mile inland. In Sri Lanka, two thousand people were killed when a passenger train was swept off its rails. Agricultural lands were severely affected, as were fishing industries. National Geographic estimated that the force of the 9.1-magnitude earthquake was stronger than 23,000 atomic bombs.

The third angel's trumpet blast causes an asteroid named wormwood to fall to earth. This will affect one-third of the rivers and springs of water, making them bitter. Many will die from the bitter waters (Rev. 8:10-11).

The fourth trumpet judgment causes one-third of the sun, moon, and stars to be darkened and not shine, day or night (Rev. 8:12). Perhaps this will be caused by volcanic clouds and ash combined with the asteroid's impact. The atmosphere is also darkened when the fifth angel opens the bottomless pit and smoke comes from the abyss, like the smoke from a great furnace (Rev. 9:1-2).

God appoints angels over specific parts of His creation to oversee it. These angels will participate in the unleashing of a specific judgment connected to their assignment. Notice the following:

- An angel over the golden altar in heaven oversees the prayers (Rev. 8:3). All the prayers of the saints are at this altar, including the martyrs who pray for God to judge and avenge their blood on those who dwell on the earth (Rev. 6:10). This angel takes incense that was offered with the prayers of the saints, fills the censer with fire from the altar, and throws it to the earth. This, in turns, empowers the seven angels to release the trumpet judgments.

- Another angel is given a key (authority) to open the bottomless pit (Rev. 9:1). It is possible that this is the same angel who descends from heaven with a chain at the end of the tribulation and casts Satan into the same abyss from which the demon locusts were released. The angel sets a seal over the pit's opening to prevent Satan from escaping from his thousand-year prison (Rev. 20:1-3).

- An angel is assigned over prophetic books (Rev. chapter 10). This angel hands a book to John and commands him to eat the book. Upon eating it, John was told to prophesy again about many people, nations, tongues, and kings. John was given more visual content to write and deliver to the churches, including an expanded understanding of Daniel's vision, the one that Daniel sealed and John was able to unseal. This included the unusual description of the final kingdom that Daniel identified as the fourth beast (Dan. 7:7-19). After eating this book, John unveiled the description of the Antichrist kingdom in Revelation 13:1-2.

- An angel is assigned to oversee the harvest of souls on the earth (Rev. 14:15). This is represented by the symbol of a large sickle in Christ's hands, and He swung the sickle over the earth to gather in the harvest, cut the grapes from the vine, and cast them into the winepress of God's wrath.

- Another angel has power over fire (Rev. 14:18). This is likely the same angel in Revelation 16:8-9 that tips a bowl judgment and releases the power of the sun to scorch men with fire. This vial that is poured out upon the sun increases the earth's temperature to the point that people will blaspheme God, knowing He is responsible for their misery.

Throughout human history as recorded in scripture, God has always used sudden and extreme environmental events as part of His chastisement or judgment against individuals or nations. This same principle seen with the Battle of Armageddon will hold true when the Islamic nations unite to battle in the northern parts of Israel during the Gog of Magog military campaign. God will defeat these armies using natural calamities that are revealed in Ezekiel's vision:

> *"And I will plead against him with pestilence and with blood; and I will rain upon him, and upon his bands, and upon the many people that are with him, an overflowing rain, and great hailstones, fire, and brimstone."*
>
> – Ezekiel 38:22 (KJV)

God will "plead against him" (Gog). This Hebrew word plead is *shaphat* and it is used in a legal sense, as when someone pleads guilty or not guilty in court and a judge orders punishment or vindication. In this case, God is acting as a defense attorney for Israel. He is saying that He will present evidence against these guilty nations that have seared consciences and hardened hearts, and who would never admit their blood guilt against the Jews and Israel.

Their judgment will be pestilence, bloodshed, floods, great hailstones, fire, and brimstone. I have been to the Bashan-Golan region over forty times, and I know the history and geography well. The area is known for its waterfalls, springs, and forests that need plenty of rain for growth. Overflowing rain and floods could give a clue about the time of year this war will occur. January is the wettest month in the Golan Heights, with an average rainfall of almost six inches. While it can rain any time from October through May, the hardest and most frequent rain falls from December through February.

It would not be unusual for the Golan to flood during the winter rain. Dams have been constructed in the Golan to prevent severe flooding in certain areas. In this battle in Ezekiel, God will use the natural element of rain to flood the armies of Gog, indicating a possible clue that the battle could occur in the winter months.

The hailstones are interesting. In the early 1990s during one of my November tours to Israel, a sudden hailstorm hit Haifa on the northern coast of Israel. It produced baseball sized hail, broke car windows, and caused damage. During Israel's winter storms, it is not uncommon for some areas to experience rain, high winds, and hail.

The third form of judgment is fire and brimstone. When Sodom and Gomorrah were destroyed, God sent fire and brimstone from heaven (Gen. 19:24). Some believe that Sodom was built near a volcano that erupted. Abraham was living at the time, and he was about forty-six miles from Sodom. He arose in the morning, looked toward Sodom, and saw smoke ascending "like the smoke of a great furnace" (Gen. 19:28). The smoke was from the cities burning, which could have been caused by volcanic activity, especially if the word "brimstone" refers to sulfur.

In 2021, at a biblical site at the north side of the Dead Sea that some now believe could be Sodom, a discovery revealed evidence of a fiery event that wiped out a city instantly. Inhabitants were likely killed within half a second. Analysis from the chemical remains indicate that the temperature briefly spiked to that of the surface of the sun. There is speculation that a meteor entered the earth's atmosphere and exploded above ground, which did not produce a crater, but it flattened and incinerated everything with the power equal to hundreds of atomic bombs. This would have been appropriately described as raining down fire and brimstone from heaven.

Fire and brimstone being connected with volcanoes is important in the Golan. Upon entering the Golan area, you will see miles and miles of black basalt stone on both sides of the road that you will not see anywhere else in Israel. This rock was formed following volcanic eruptions when the ash and rock solidified. The Golan Heights is a plateau of basalt, and there are over sixty volcanic hills in the area that formed after volcanic eruptions. A field of dormant volcanoes extends as far as Damascus. What could cause a resurgence in volcanic activity and bring fire and brimstone upon the armies of Gog?

One answer could be an earthquake of 6.0-magnitude or higher. Under certain conditions, such an earthquake can trigger a volcano, and a volcanic eruption can also trigger an earthquake. In Chili in the 1960s, a 9.5-magnitude earthquake was followed by a volcanic eruption less than two days later. On July 29, 2025, an 8.8-magnitude earthquake occurred in the North Pacific, off the coast of Russia. Days later, a volcano less than 150 miles away from the earthquake epicenter erupted for the first time in hundreds of years. This was followed by the eruption of five more volcanoes.

How could a similar scenario play into the Gog of Magog War? God Himself explained to Ezekiel the key component to breaking Gog's power:

> *"And it will come to pass at the same time, when Gog comes against the land of Israel," says the Lord God, "that My fury will show in My face. For in My jealousy and in the fire of My wrath I have spoken: 'Surely in that day there shall be a great earthquake in the land of Israel, so that the fish of the sea, the birds of the heavens, the beasts of the field, all creeping things that creep on the earth, and all men who are on the face of the earth shall shake at My presence. The mountains shall be thrown down, the steep places shall fall, and every wall shall fall to the ground."*
>
> – EZEKIEL 38:18-29 (NKJV)

The Almighty makes it clear that when the armies arrive, there will be a great earthquake in the land of Israel. This "great shaking" (KJV) will be so powerful, it will be felt throughout Israel. The fish in the sea will feel the effects. The two bodies of water linked with Israel that have fish are the Sea of Galilee to the south of the Golan, and the Mediterranean Sea, whose coastline is a straight-line distance of around forty miles from the edge of the Golan Heights.

Birds and animals (beasts of the field) are naturally sensitive to changes in their environment and seem to have a heightened sensitivity to impending disasters such as earthquakes and tsunamis. Their behaviors change. Birds might suddenly leave nesting areas, reverse their flight pattern or fly very low to the ground, and become silent. Animals often become noticeably restless. Scientists don't understand why this happens, but perhaps it is because animals have a heightened sense of smell, and they hear frequencies that are inaudible to humans. This allows them to notice things in the environment that humans cannot observe, such as noise produced by tectonic movements that humans would not know are happening until the earthquake occurred. In the Golan Heights, cattle are raised for both dairy and beef. God told Ezekiel that these beasts of the field will shake at His presence.

This will be a severe earthquake as indicated by walls collapsing and mountains being affected to the point of changing the landscape of the region. There are "steep places" throughout the Golan, including canyons, some with rock overlooks that offer amazing views. The possibilities of rain, hail, earthquakes, and volcanic activity are all present in the Golan Heights, where northern armies will descend like a cloud against Israel.

WHY A WINTER WAR?

This is only speculation, but perhaps one of the reasons the Gog invasion could occur in the winter has to do with satellite imagery. In winter, the Golan can experience extreme cloud covering, which significantly hinders satellites from relaying quality imagery back to the station. Some of this can be overcome with new technologies, perhaps radar or infrared imagery.

Of course, we cannot ignore other factors that could affect both satellite imagery, modern military equipment, and military movement. Geomagnetic storms, solar flares, signal jamming and various forms of interference, cyberattacks, and other such things could cause military disruptions. Almost everything in our modern world operates with technology that is susceptible to hacking and electronic tampering. Consider the kinds of attacks that can or already have occurred against our infrastructure and think how that might affect military maneuverability and readiness.

We could speculate on the reasons why an army might attack Israel from the north during the winter, and we could speculate about the reasons a military response might be hindered. Extreme cold, excessive rain, fog, and terrain could hinder tanks and some technology. But considering that Israel has such advanced tanks and weaponry, there could be other reasons why an army chooses to attack in the winter. It might have more to do with the timing of technology disruptions than the season of the year.

Ezekiel saw the armies coming on horses and horseback. In Ezekiel's time, 2,500 years ago, there were only three ways to invade another nation: an army of foot soldiers, an army riding horses and chariots, and an army coming by ship at sea.

Critics of the Ezekiel vision believe that this prophecy was an early battle or just a ridiculous vision, as no army fights on horseback today. One rebuttal to that argument is that this might be the way God chose to reveal to an early prophet that war is coming. How would Ezekiel describe, for example, a helicopter? Would he call it a flying locust? What about a military tank? He might see such a vehicle as a large beast, like a chariot, with fire coming from its nostril.

The second rebuttal is that some countries use horses in battle for certain military roles. Rugged terrain is one reason for using horses. In Afghanistan in 2001, U.S. Special Forces rode horses to fight the Taliban. Horses are used in Afghan fighting because they can navigate the rugged and mountainous terrain. An army descending from the north into Israel in the winter months would have to cross rugged terrain and snow-covered mountains. Let's consider other reasons why an army might choose to invade Israel from the north in the rainy season and the middle of winter, and why they might choose to do so on horseback.

One cannot help but consider the effects of an electromagnetic pulse weapon (EMP). These bursts of electromagnetic radiation, if used in war or to destroy an enemy's weapons and infrastructure, are highly destructive to everything electronic. The EMP is a nuclear explosion at a high altitude, and it will destroy modern electronic infrastructure. It does not necessarily kill people right away, but it will be a grave danger to long term human survival. Non-nuclear electromagnetic pulse weapons can also be used to significantly damage a localized region. It's possible to picture a scenario where non-nuclear EMPs could do enough damage to catch even the best military off guard and cause a delayed response to an attack. It could disable communications, jam networks and tanks, destroy radar, disable naval ships, shut down computer systems, and so on.

If the nations that come against Israel have experienced the same attacks against their military, they also will be without modern weapons. If they suspect that Israel was involved, they will act in retaliation. This would make the scenario of destroying Israel's communications and invading on horseback, even in the winter, entirely plausible.

Combine that with food shortages that are the likely *hook in the jaws* trigger (Ezekiel 38:4), and we paint a picture of why an army attacks from both the north and the east. The climate is diverse enough in Israel that they still can grow food in the winter, especially citrus fruits. Each region has its own distinct conditions for growing different types of food throughout the year.

It doesn't matter so much about the weapons and type of warfare that Israel's enemies choose. They're doomed regardless, because when the "natural disasters" hit them all at once, God will knock the bow out of their left hand and their arrows out of their right hand (Ezek. 39:3). Whatever weapons the enemies use will become useless. With an earthquake, floods, large hail, and volcanic activity, it is not an exaggeration to say that five out of six soldiers will be slain.

DINNER FOR THE BIRDS OF PREY

Ezekiel noted that the enemies of Israel will be given to the birds of prey and beasts of the field to be devoured:

> *"You shall fall upon the mountains of Israel, you and all your troops and the peoples who are with you; I will give you to birds of prey of every sort and to the beasts of the field to be devoured. You shall fall on the open field; for I have spoken," says the Lord GOD."*
>
> – Ezekiel 39:4-5 (NKJV)

In the early 1990s we were touring northern Israel in the Golan Heights with my tour guide, Gideon Shor. He took our group to a park with a large canyon located north of the Sea of Galilee. There we saw large birds with a wingspan of seven to nine feet flying above the canyon. These are called Griffon vultures and they feed on carcasses. They are found in the mountains of the Golan, the upper Galilee, and the Judean and Negev deserts.

The Gamla Nature Reserve in the Golan Heights is a breeding and nesting area for these vultures. They have been on the endangered species list in Israel, especially after many of them were found dead from poisoning in 2019. Conservation measures, such as captive breeding and release, have been implemented to increase their population. Besides vultures, other birds of prey that pass through Israel include eagles, hawks, falcons, buzzards, and kites.

The primary migration seasons in Israel for birds of prey are March through May, and again from August to November. Over a million birds of prey pass through Israel annually. They concentrate in great numbers around Mt. Hermon and the Hula Valley in the north, and the Eilat Bird Sanctuary in southern Israel.

In the Golan Heights is an ancient megalithic structure made of 42,000 concentric basalt rocks with a burial space underneath. Together the rocks weigh more than 40,000 tons. In Arabic this structure is called Rujm el-Hiri, meaning "stone heap of the wild cat." In Hebrew it is called Gilgal Refaim, which means "wheel of the giants."

Archaeologists date this structure to the 3rd millennium BC. Some archaeologists say that an ancient culture placed the bodies of the deceased on these stones and allowed birds of prey to pick flesh off the carcass, so that they could later bury only the skeletal remains.

There will be many corpses after the War of Gog of Magog, and they will remain in the open fields because an organized burial does not begin until seven months following the war. Will they choose to leave the bodies where they fell until the flesh is devoured? I am not suggesting that bodies of the deceased will be placed on the stones of this ancient structure for birds to pick the carcasses clean. But the historical repetition in the same area is interesting, since the Bible tells us that Israel's enemies will be devoured by birds of prey and beasts of the field.

CHAPTER 19

KINGS OF THE EAST AND 1.5 BILLION HINDUS

Since the 1980s I have made over forty trips to Israel, and those trips have expanded my prophetic understanding in new ways. Most people in the United States who have never been to Israel and don't understand Israel's prophetic future will study and teach end-time prophecy from the spiritual and political viewpoint of a western mind. The western viewpoint means that every prophecy must be connected to the church or to the political framework of America. Once a person visits the Middle East and observes its politics, religions, and people up close, a biblically literate person will begin to reevaluate certain western prophetic interpretations.

When I was a teenager, the common belief about the Antichrist was that he would be a Jew from Israel, and specifically from the tribe of Dan. This is never stated in scripture, but it was based on some theological suppositions. It was assumed that, because Jesus was Jewish and from Israel, the future Antichrist would have to be Jewish and from Israel.

My tours to Israel caused me to ask myself this question: There are about fifteen million Jews in the world and at least a billion and a half Muslims. Israel is surrounded by Islamic nations. Why is nobody talking about the role of Muslims in the last days?

Then many years ago, an Iranian lady who attended one of my services heard me preach a message about end-times prophecy. After the church service, she explained to me the Islamic belief regarding the Mahdi, an eschatological figure that the Muslims expect to return at the end of times to set the world straight.

As I took that information, researched further, and searched the scriptures, I realized that the Antichrist will be a Gentile. The end-time Gentile kingdom will come out of an Islamic nation, and the beast will rise from the area of the Mediterranean Sea. A Jew has no need to take over Jerusalem, as Israel already possesses the city. A Jew would not kill Jews in Jerusalem and build an image for people to worship, as worshipping an image is against all Jewish and biblical teaching. This research led to me write about the possibility of an Islamic Antichrist in the books, *Unleashing the Beast* and *The Eighth Kingdom*.

I was sitting with a great apostolic leader, Dr. Jim Marocco, who directs hundreds of churches worldwide. We were talking about the different theories concerning the background of the Antichrist and his religions. Dr. Marocco pointed out something I have not heard discussed in all my decades of ministering in prophetic circles. He was born in Calcutta, India where he was raised in a boarding school for missionary children. He is very familiar with the culture, political views, and religious beliefs of the country and the Hindu religion.

As we discussed end-time prophetic events, Dr. Marocco noted that India is east of Israel and has a huge population. In fact, India's population has surpassed 1.46 billion people, outranking China as the most populous country in the world. India is the seventh largest nation in terms of land mass. Over 1.1 billion people in India practice the Hindu religion.

Militarily, of the top ten countries with the largest active-duty military, India ranks second, with over 1.45 million active-duty military personnel. China ranks number one, with over two million active-duty military personnel. When we think of a military, we don't think of

India; however, their active-duty personnel outnumber even that of the United States.

Considering all this, Dr. Marocco concluded that India certainly must play some kind of significant role in end-times prophecy. This made me wonder if perhaps India will be part of the "kings of the east" who will march from the east toward Israel at the time of the end.

> "And the sixth angel poured out his vial upon the great river Euphrates; and the water thereof was dried up, that the way of the kings of the east might be prepared."
>
> – Revelation 16:12 (KJV)

The entire Armageddon army is believed to be two hundred million strong, if we consider Revelation 9:16. In that part of the world, it would not be difficult to gather two hundred million men to go to war. The question is, how will they get there?

THE NEW SILK ROAD

The silk road was an ancient four-thousand-mile web of caravan trading routes that connected China with Asia, the Middle East, and Europe. Trade began there in the 2nd century BC and lasted until the Roman Empire collapsed and the Arabs took control. The Mongols revived trade along the silk road in the 13th century, and part of the road connecting China and Pakistan still exists today. People carried more than silk and wool, oil and perfume, and gold and silver along the silk road. They traded their cultures, religions, and even their diseases. It is believed that trade caravans from Asia were responsible for the Black Plague that killed tens of millions of people in Europe.

In 2012, China announced a new infrastructure project to connect multiple continents. They call it the Belt and Road Initiative, the One Belt One Road Initiative, or the New Silk Road. This Chinese led investment project aims to improve connectivity, trade, and communications across the same ancient lands, plus Africa and Latin America. China has lent over $1 trillion to other countries to construct or upgrade highways, railways, natural gas plants, solar power plants, port projects, and such. Some projects have failed and left developing countries with a debt they cannot repay to China. Over 150 countries have signed an agreement to participate with China in this initiative, which might help explain why so many countries have become invested in China's success to the detriment of their own nations.

Under this Belt and Road initiative, a new railroad became operational this year that seamlessly connects China with Kazakhstan, Turkmenistan, Uzbekistan, Iran, and Turkey. In May of 2025, the first train left central China and traveled the China-Iran railway corridor, arriving at an Iranian port on the Persian Gulf fifteen days later. It bypassed all oceans and maritime routes and shortened delivery time by half or more. The land route that took fifteen days would normally take thirty to forty days by sea.

This railroad covers 7,500 miles of territory. The trip to Iran in May covered 6,000 miles. As of now, this train carries freight only, but China has mentioned their desire to expand the rail to carry passengers as well.

Countries that border China include India, Pakistan, Afghanistan, Tajikistan, Kyrgyzstan, and Kazakhstan. Countries that share a border with Iran include Pakistan, Afghanistan, Turkmenistan, Azerbaijan, Turkey, and Iraq, with Syria nestled between Turkey and Iraq.

The Euphrates River, where the armies will eventually cross, runs through Turkey, Syria, and Iraq, where it empties into the Persian Gulf, not far from Iran. Except for China and India, every country listed is predominantly Muslim. All countries listed, including China and India, have a combined population of three-and-a-half billion people.

Considering the access these countries have to China's New Silk Road, perhaps many of the soldiers will be brought to the area by train, as well as other forms of transportation as they plan their march toward Armageddon.

As mentioned, India is predominately a Hundi nation and Pakistan is predominantly Muslim. Their dispute over the Kashmir region has its roots in religious tension, which resulted in the Muslims wanting a homeland. Pakistan was created as a separate country for Muslims in 1947. The complicated explanation of their battles over Kashmir is not necessary for this chapter, but the point is that there is constant military, political, and spiritual tension between nations, people, and political leaders.

With so much of this area north and east of Israel being Islamic, under the Antichrist's rule, will he and his ten nations control farmland, oil fields, transportation, and lands that are in dispute? The answer is emphatically yes. How will the Hindus in India react to being under the control of Islamic rulers? India must feed nearly 1.5 billion people, at a time when land will be polluted, water will be undrinkable, and food shortages will be common. During the tribulation, up to two-thirds of the world's population will perish, so India's numbers will likely be greatly reduced. Still, it is worth pondering the most populous nation on earth, its centralized location to end-time prophetic events, and the part that India might play during the rule of the Antichrist.

CHAPTER 20

DOES THE BIBLE HINT OF NUCLEAR WAR?

Years ago, a minister friend and I were discussing end-time prophecy and researching scripture for any concealed clues that might hint at the use of nuclear weapons in future wars. He had many Jewish contacts and friends in Israel, and one military commander pointed him to these verses in Joel:

> *"And I will shew wonders in the heavens and in the earth, blood, and fire, and pillars of smoke. The sun shall be turned into darkness, and the moon into blood, before the great and the terrible day of the Lord come."*
>
> – Joel 2:30-31 (KJV)

The phrase "fire and pillars of smoke" is commonly interpreted as eruptions of numerous volcanoes at the same time around the globe, which are part of Joel's "signs in the earth beneath." The Israeli commander noted that Joel 2:30 uses a specific Hebrew word for pillars. The word is *timarah*, and it means "a column, a cloud, like a palm tree." The commander noted that a palm tree spreads out at the top in the same form of a mushroom-shaped nuclear cloud. The trunk of the palm tree, like the nuclear explosion, rises from the ground like a long, round column.

The smoke from the explosion is blood red. This imagery might seem a bit of a stretch, but we know that in this world, a nuclear threat is ever present and real.

NATIONS WITH NUCLEAR WEAPONS

Here is a list of nuclear nations and the total number of nuclear warheads in their arsenal, according to World Population Review:

- Russia: 5,459
- United States: 5,177
- China: 600
- France: 290
- United Kingdom: 225
- Pakistan: 170
- India: 180
- Israel: 90
- North Korea: 50

Some countries use nuclear weapons as a deterrent strategy or to control retaliation from other countries. Notice the nations on the list that presently are at war or have been involved in dangerous border clashes. Notice the nations whose leaders sometimes threaten to use weapons of mass destruction against their enemies.

While this book was being written, the Russia-Ukraine war was still going on. The chair of Russia's Security Council has threatened to use a nuclear weapon if they feel their existence is threatened and if the attack against Russia is supported by NATO countries with nuclear weapons.

In April of 2025, terrorists from Pakistan entered Kashmir, which is under the administration of India, and massacred twenty-six tourists who were mostly Hindu. In retaliation, India halted water flow to Pakistan, and Pakistan viewed the violation of their water treaty as an act of war. A battle escalated between India and Pakistan, both of which have an arsenal of nuclear weapons. The fighting stopped after the U.S. brokered a cease-fire on May 10.

North Korea, also a nuclear country, enjoys testing their ballistic missiles and threatening other countries, especially South Korea, with the use of nuclear weapons. North Korea's leadership is not open to dialogue with any of the countries they threaten.

Intelligence sources have been aware for many years that Iran has been enriching uranium and had the capability, at any time, to turn their enriched uranium into nuclear warheads, thus threatening not just Israel and the Middle East, but much of the world. Their Islamic radical leaders had threatened to use their future nuclear arsenal to destroy the "little Satan" (Israel) and the "big Satan" (America). In one night, the U.S. military was able to bomb Iran's deep underground nuclear facilities and set back Iran's nuclear capabilities for the foreseeable future.

Nuclear weapons in the hands of a rogue leader, a radical Islamic dictator, or terrorists is something that keeps military experts awake at night.

WHAT HAPPENS IN A NUCLEAR ATTACK?

The Department of Homeland Security issued a nuclear attack fact sheet that is publicly available on their website. They explain that a terrorist could carry out an attack with an improvised nuclear device using components from stolen weapons or by using plutonium or highly enriched uranium. It is not easy to obtain nuclear materials because the weapons and components are carefully inventoried and guarded. They are also heavy, weighing from a few hundred pounds to several tons, so they are not easily transported.

A nuclear weapon can be dropped from an airplane or by shooting a ballistic missile from the ground. It is called a ground blast when detonated on or slightly above the ground, and it produces intense heat, light, air pressure, and radiation. Radioactive particles are drawn up into a mushroom cloud and the fallout can be experienced from several miles to hundreds of miles away. The ionization of the atmosphere around the blast drives electrical current through underground wires and causes damage.

The initial impact will cause death or injuries to those in the explosion vicinity, either from the fireball (which can reach tens of millions of degrees), the thermal heat energy, the powerful energy from the shockwave, falling debris, or falling buildings. Depending on the weapon design and the altitude of the explosion, the energy released by a nuclear explosion is distributed roughly as fifty percent shockwave, thirty-five percent heat, five percent initial nuclear radiation, and ten percent fallout radiation.

Acute radiation syndrome will develop in those who are exposed to certain levels of radiation. Depending on their level of exposure, people could die within hours or days, or within weeks or months from various medical conditions. Those who survive long term are at increased risk of developing cancer.

A nuclear weapon that is detonated in the upper atmosphere, known as an electromagnetic pulse weapon, gives a different result. An EMP is a burst of electromagnetic energy produced by a nuclear explosion in the atmosphere. These cause widespread damage to power lines, telecommunications, electronic equipment, and critical infrastructure such as transportation, banking, financial systems, and emergency services. That leads to severe disruptions of daily life, as almost everything today depends on electronics and computers to operate.

The atomic bombs dropped on Hiroshima and Nagasaki, Japan in August 1945 were detonated 1,600 feet above the ground. At Hiroshima, buildings were destroyed over a four-square-mile radius, and 60,000 people died instantly. Within two to four months, the death toll was estimated to be 90,000 to 140,000.

An even larger bomb was dropped at the same altitude on Nagasaki, and 60,000 to 80,000 died immediately. The years following, many survivors suffered from cancer, attributed to the radiation exposure.

The possibility of a high-altitude detonation of a nuclear weapon has been discussed by most governments, as the ramifications of this type of electromagnetic pulse attack is feared by nearly every world leader and their military agencies. A detonation above a large urban city would send a powerful pulse of energy that would disrupt jobs, school, transportation, communication, water supplies, and almost everything vital to daily life. The disruptions could last weeks, months, or years, although most affected people would die before years passed.

Imagine the horror of being within the deadly radius of a nuclear ground detonation. With a fireball that can reach tens of millions of degrees, death would be instant for some and unbearably painful for the rest. The surface of the sun is about ten thousand degrees Fahrenheit, and an average house fire can reach up to 1,500 degrees Fahrenheit. Just imagine being in the vicinity of a ground nuclear explosion.

Depending on the amount of uranium or plutonium in the weapons, it could take from one year to many years for the area to be cleaned up and inhabitable again.

EZEKIEL'S VISION—MILITARY CAMPAIGN (EZEKIEL 38-39)

At the present time, the nations that will organize to march against Israel in the Gog of Magog war do not have nuclear weapons. Ezekiel 39:14 has puzzled scholars and led them to believe that the seven-month delay in burying the dead is because of contamination that was caused by chemical, biological, or small nuclear weapons. This is not to say that a nuclear device will be used, but it is possible.

Several factors determine how quickly cleanup can happen and how soon the land becomes inhabitable again. Primarily it depends on the type and size of the bomb and whether it was an air or ground detonation. Air detonation causes less radiation fallout on the ground, while ground detonation causes heavy radiation fallout. Cleanup can begin in one to six months. Resettlement could take up to five years, or even decades if the fallout was heavy. Some places might never be inhabitable again.

The puzzling Ezekiel verses read:

> *"And they shall sever out men of continual employment, passing through the land to bury with the passengers those that remain upon the face of the earth, to cleanse it: after the end of seven months shall they search."*
>
> – Ezekiel 39:14 (KJV)

> *"And seven months shall the house of Israel be burying of them, that they may cleanse the land."*
>
> – Ezekiel 39:12 (KJV)

This description sounds as though Ezekiel could be describing cleanup after the detonation of a small nuclear device. This effects of even a low radiation nuclear weapon are reason enough to keep these weapons out of the hands of terrorists, and to be concerned when a nuclear armed country threatens to use them on other countries. With the condition of the nations before the return of Christ, we can be reasonably certain that the world will see the use of nuclear weapons.

CHRIST BRINGING DESTRUCTION BY FIRE

The prophet Zechariah described a plague that will be placed upon the people who fought against Jerusalem:

> "And this shall be the plague with which the LORD will strike all the people who fought against Jerusalem: their flesh shall dissolve while they stand on their feet, their eyes shall dissolve in their sockets, and their tongues shall dissolve in their mouths. It shall come to pass in that day that a great panic from the LORD will be among them. Everyone will seize the hand of his neighbor, and raise his hand against his neighbor's hand..."
>
> – ZECHARIAH 14:12-13 (NKJV)

The Hebrew word *plague* was often used to describe a pestilence God allowed to strike Israel when they resisted His warnings to repent, or to enemy nations who attacked God's people without a cause. The most well-known biblical examples were the ten plagues that struck Egypt, each of which represented ten of Egypt's many gods. The Bible did not refer to this as a weapon, but a method of divine retribution against Egypt's treatment of His people. Zechariah continued:

> "Such also shall be the plague on the horse and the mule, on the camel and the donkey, And on all the cattle that will be in those camps. So shall this plague be."
>
> – ZECHARIAH 14:15 (NKJV)

When this prophecy comes to pass, the flesh of all humans and animals will be consumed instantly. Some military experts I have spoken with have said the weaponry exists that would do exactly what is written in scripture. These are thermonuclear weapons that release a high level of radiation with a small blast. The weapon instantly kills people and all living creatures in a smaller, confined area, but damage to structures is minimal. A Christian colonel who was familiar with various types of weapons expressed his opinion that, when this event occurs, he believes it is the brightness of Christ's return that causes this reaction, as Paul wrote that the people would be destroyed with the brightness of Christ return..." These verses are found in First Thessalonians:

> "Seeing it is a righteous thing with God to recompense tribulation to them that trouble you; And to you who are troubled rest with us, when the Lord Jesus shall be revealed from heaven with his mighty angels, in flaming fire taking vengeance on them that know not God, and that obey not the gospel of our Lord Jesus Christ: Who shall be punished with everlasting destruction from the presence of the Lord, and from the glory of his power."
>
> – 2 Thessalonians 1:6-9 (KJV)

> "And then the lawless one will be revealed, whom the Lord will consume with the breath of His mouth and destroy with the brightness of His coming."
>
> – 2 Thessalonians 2:8 (NKJV)

The brightness of His coming could indeed physically destroy the wicked in Christ's path. He will return to save Israel, defeat the world's armies, bind Satan, and remove the Antichrist, False Prophet, and all who have taken the mark of the beast from the earth.

LYING SPIRITS LIKE FROGS

In the book of Revelation, John saw three unclean spirits that looked like frogs, and they used the mouths of the False Prophet, the Antichrist, and his beast kingdom to deceive people and organize them for battle

(Rev. 16:13-14). They will incite the world's armies to gather in the Valley of Jezreel, also named the Valley of Megiddo, for the battle of Armageddon. The influence of these three demonic spirits is evident as they successfully pull the nations to battle (Rev. 16:16).

In Revelation 16:12, John also spoke of the "kings from the east." These are a group of leaders who unite the eastern powers to form a massive coalition. Two of these nations are likely to be China and India, considering that both are populous countries with a large military force and an arsenal of nuclear weapons.

Then we have India and Pakistan. Both are nuclear nations that have been at odds with each other since 1947 when the British partitioned India, and the Indian leader of the Muslim-majority state of Kashmir chose to join India instead of the newly established Pakistan.

The eastern kings will lead a massive army toward Armageddon in the future. Then Christ will come in flaming fire to take vengeance on those who do not know God and have not obeyed the gospel (2 Thess. 1:7-9).

THE DESTRUCTION OF MYSTERY BABYLON

The Apocalypse alludes to a *great* city ("megas" in Greek, meaning exceedingly large and strong) that rules over the kings of the earth. John identified the city as a harlot riding a beast. In Revelation chapters 17 and 18, John concealed the name of the city with the title, "Mystery Babylon."

When he penned this book, John was a political prisoner of Rome on the desolate island of Patmos. God revealed future events to John in a series of visions, and He concealed the interpretation of the prophecies using various symbols, including animal symbolism. Most scholars believe that Mystery Babylon is the city of Rome, which in John's time was persecuting Christians and ruling much of the known world. Had

John exposed Rome as the city, his scroll of revelation would have been burned by the Roman soldiers and he could have been slain.

The empires of Rome and Babylon had several parallels:

- both invaded Jerusalem
- both seized the Temple treasures
- both burned the gates and the Temple with fire
- both took the Jewish people captive
- both destroyed the Temple on the 9th of Av
- both left a small remnant in the land.

Another clue that this city could be Rome is that John said the city was drunken with the blood of the saints and with the blood of the martyrs of Jesus (Rev. 17:6). This alludes to Roman soldiers at the crucifixion, their beheading of Paul, and their intense persecution of believers.

John said that the ten king coalition of the Antichrist hated the city and would burn it with fire. The utter destruction would come in one day (Rev. 18:8, 16, 17). In AD 64, Rome burned for over a week from the fire the Emperor Nero is believed to have started, even though much of the city was stone and marble. The burning that John saw in the vision happens quickly, with ships remaining off at a distance and people weeping and wailing as they see the destructive smoke rising in the air (Rev. 18:15-19).

> "Therefore, shall her plagues come in one day, death, and mourning, and famine; and she shall be utterly burned with fire: for strong is the Lord God who judges her."
>
> – REVELATION 18:8

DANGEROUS RELIGIOUS BELIEFS AND DEADLY WEAPONS

The Hindu and Islamic religions have beliefs that could permit them to use nuclear weapons in the future without fear of eternal retribution. In India, the Hindus believe in the cycle of reincarnation, in which the soul of the deceased is continually reborn into a new body, until the soul achieves liberation. According to Hinduism, the soul of a person with "bad karma" could be reborn into suffering or lower life forms.

With the belief in reincarnation, death to a Hindu is just another cycle of life. This idea is interesting in terms of a destructive war, because of the belief that those who die will simply return as someone or something else. If a Hindu leader were to detonate nuclear weapons, his ideology of recycling the soul could be used as reasoning to take such action.

Islamic radicals believe that if they die in a holy war (jihad) against infidels (non-Muslims), they are guaranteed entrance to paradise. The men also believe they will be given seventy-two perpetual virgins if they kill the enemies of Islam. Journalists and defectors have reported that radical Islamic leaders have sent young boys across land to clear mines, placing plastic keys around their necks and telling them that, if they die in a mine explosion, the key will be their entry to paradise as martyrs.

Paradise is a central theme in all branches of Islam, and the promise of paradise includes good works. However, this idea of automatic entry to paradise after dying as a jihad martyr is primarily a radical Islamic idea. This is one reason why suicide bombings were so prevalent at one time, especially in Israel.

Since Islamic terrorists believe that murdering infidels guarantees them an eternity of pleasure in a heavenly paradise, young men have a willingness to die martyrs. For a jihadist, the use of a nuclear device is just a faster path to a place they falsely believe to be their eternal destination.

Another dangerous person is a ruthless and sadistic dictator. When such a person knows that his death could soon be on the horizon, why would he care about releasing weapons of mass destruction? He will die anyway, at which time he cannot suffer arrest or retaliation. It was once said that a leader overseeing war with another nation was suffering from cancer and would die soon, and as his final act of defiance, he planned to use nuclear missiles to decimate an enemy nation. Thankfully, that did not happen.

THE SIGN OF FIRE

According to Islamic apocalyptic beliefs, a sign that the last days and the Day of Judgment have arrived will be fire from heaven. They believe a fire will come from the region of Hejaz in western Saudi Arabia, an area that also includes Mecca and Medina, the two most important cities of Islam. They believe that the light of this fire from heaven will be so bright, it will illuminate the sky and be seen hundreds of miles away in other countries. They believe there will also be a fire coming from under the earth. This could be volcanic in nature.

The Antichrist's religion will likely be Islam or a mixture of Islamic beliefs and other religious ideologies, including apostate Christianity. Many Catholic teachers and theologians now accept the theory that the coming False Prophet who will perform false miracles is likely an apostate pope. Some refer to him as a "defective" Pope. The symbol of the False Prophet is the same symbol used for Christ throughout the New Testament—a lamb (with two horns)."

> *"He performs great signs, so that he even makes fire come down from heaven on the earth in the sight of men. And he deceives those who dwell on the earth—by those signs which he was granted to do in the sight of the beast..."*
>
> – REVELATION 13:13-14 (NKJV)

Does the Bible Hint of Nuclear War?

By the time the tribulation events reach Revelation 13, the Antichrist and False Prophet have transferred their headquarters to Jerusalem, where both will rule over their ten-nation coalition for a final forty-two months. If the False Prophet is a defective Pope who attempts to dominate over two religions (two horns: apostate Christianity and Islam), with his headquarters in Jerusalem, a place considered sacred to Jews, Muslims and Christians, there will be no need for a headquarters in Italy for Rome and the Vatican.

The question becomes, is this *fire from heaven* an order given under the direction of the False Prophet to annihilate Rome with fire through some type of nuclear weapon?

There appear to be hints in the Bible that some prophetic verses signify the use of highly destructive modern weapons. Other verses indicate that some of the fire is spiritual in nature, especially when connected with the return of Christ.

CHAPTER 21

THE PROPHECY — WHEN AMERICA STOPS PROTECTING ISRAEL

Ten years ago, nobody would have believed it if someone told them that people living in the United States would become anti-Semitic and anti-Israel, attack Jewish students on Ivy League university campuses, support Islamic terrorism, and demand that the Jewish people be removed from Israel and the land handed over to the Palestinians. After the invasion by Hamas on October 7th, 2023, we would assume that Israelis who saw their citizens attacked, slain, kidnapped, and tortured to death would have received sympathy and support.

Instead, right here in the United States of America, mobs of young people and adults (many from Islamic countries) praised the terrorists and condemned Israel and the Jewish people for responding to the attacks. Since the Hamas attacks, the majority of Jewish adults have reported experiencing antisemitism, and an equal number feel less safe in America.

We have seen an increasing demand that the United States stop supporting Israel. Is it possible, at some time in the future, that the United States will no longer support Israel?

Believers who are familiar with Bible prophecy sometimes ask: Is America found in biblical prophecy? What is America's end-time role?

God is the greatest mathematician and pattern creator, and He uses numbers, colors, symbolism, types and shadows, cycles, patterns, and parallels to conceal His mysteries, including prophetic secrets. Certainly, America is not mentioned by name, nor is it alluded to in scripture. However, America does have government parallels to the ancient Roman Republic and spiritual parallels to ancient Israel. The only time the west is alluded to in biblical prophecy is in the book of Daniel, when he noted the rise of the He-Goat coming from the west, which was Greece and Alexander the Great.

THE EZEKIEL NATIONS

As Ezekiel detailed the nations involved in the Gog of Magog War, he also listed the names of those who would not be involved, but who seemingly sit back and question the reasoning behind the invasion.

> *"Sheba, Dedan, the merchants of Tarshish, and all their young lions will say to you, 'Have you come to take plunder? Have you gathered your army to take booty, to carry away silver and gold, to take away livestock and goods, to take great plunder?"*
>
> – Ezekiel 38:13 (NKJV)

Most early biblical names can be identified with modern nations. Some prophetic nations have maintained the same name since biblical times, although the borders of these nations have changed. Other biblical names and their current locations are debated by scholars.

Recall the story of the Queen of Sheba, a wealthy African queen who visited Solomon and presented him with elaborate and expensive gifts (1 Kings 10). The name Sheba was also given to three men in scripture (Gen. 10:7; 25:3; 2 Sam. 20). Biblical scholars are divided on the location of Sheba in Ezekiel 38:13, with some suggesting it was an area in Northern Africa, perhaps Ethiopia, while others suggest it was a land on the Arabian Peninsula.

Ezekiel mentions Dedan. In scripture, Dedan was one of Abraham's grandsons through his wife Keturah, the woman he married after Sarah died (Gen. 25:1-3). The land of Dedan is believed to be in northwestern Saudi Arabia, a place in ancient history that was known for caravans and trade.

Ezekiel 38 mentions a third name, Tarshish. There are several opinions on today's location of Tarshish. One theory is that it is an area in southern Spain, which in early times was a trade center. Others believe it could be Tarsus, located in southern Turkey. It also could be a region to the west of Israel, as far away as Britain.

The idea of Tarshish being connected with Britain is due to the phrase, "and all their young lions." These young lions are somehow connected to Tarshish. The lion is a symbol of British history that dates back to Richard the Lionheart. The lion, a symbol of national pride, appears on the Royal Coat of Arms, military insignias, and passports. Traditionally, the lion is considered a symbol of Britain.

One theory of the "young lions" suggests that, because the lion can symbolize Britain and the United States was formed out of Britain, that makes the United States one of the "young lions." Other nations were once under the British Empire as well.

There are simply too many theories, and it cannot be determined which one is correct. However, the lion and young lion symbolism could fit the British — America theory.

THE POLITICAL DIVIDE

Currently we are witnessing a great political divide in the United States over our unwavering support for Israel. After the holocaust photos were released and Americans realized the horrible atrocities committed by the Nazi regime, including the deaths of six million Jews, most Americans were supportive of a Jewish state in their original homeland.

An earlier chapter of this book explained the history of wars between Israel and their Arab neighbors, and how the idea of a separate Palestinian state plays into many conflicts. That conflict has caused many Palestinians in the region to think that Israel is occupying land that belongs to Palestinian Arabs.

Pew Research and Gallup polls conducted in 2025 indicate that over half of Americans now hold an unfavorable view of Israel. Gallup says this is their lowest polling number since the year 2000. Polls show that sixty-nine percent of Democrats hold an unfavorable view of Israel, with some Democrat members of Congress standing in solidarity alongside pro-Hamas protestors and against the Jewish state. Republicans hold a thirty-seven percent unfavorable view of Israel, which is up from twenty-seven percent three years ago, while Independents poll at forty-four percent unfavorable toward Israel. Younger adults hold the most unfavorable view, with ninety percent being especially critical of Israel.

We have also witnessed anti-Israel Muslims moving into U.S. cities, where they are being elected to school boards, city councils, mayoral positions, state governments, and Congress. The more influence the anti-Israel contingent gains, the more opposition we will witness to Israel and even to Jewish people living in the United States.

THE YEARS 2028 TO 2032

America's election results seem to run in cycles. People elect leaders that are far to the left, then four to eight years later, they change their minds and choose leaders who are more conservative. Four to eight years later, they swing the pendulum back to the far left and choose leaders who undo everything the conservative leaders attempted to accomplish.

The next two U.S. presidential and congressional elections held in 2028 and 2032 will determine whether future U.S. administrations will support or turn their backs on Israel. For almost five decades I have studied biblical prophecy, and considering the fulfillment of prophetic events that we are currently witnessing, I will say with confidence that these two election cycles will be very important in terms of prophetic fulfillment. The action we take in these years will help determine both the political and spiritual direction of the United States. We could see more prophetic wars and the rise of the future beast kingdom. This will be a significant timeframe for nations of the world, and for the United States especially.

WHY AMERICA MIGHT NOT BE INVOLVED

America's military support or involvement, or lack thereof, in the future invasion of Israel by Islamic nations will be based on circumstances unknown at this time. Several factors could affect the decision.

1. The administration that is in power at the time

When the sound of marching hordes is heard across the mountains of Israel, America's support will be determined by the President and leadership of the United States at the time. I have heard discussions among Muslims about an eschatological prophecy in the Hadith about the arrival of the day of judgment that states, "The hour will not come until the sun rises from the west." Some consider this literal, while others say it is symbolic. To some, the sun will literally have to rise in the west. To others, especially those from the Middle East, it means that the "light of Islam" will rise in the west—that is, Islam will rise in western countries. One Muslim told me that, one day, America will have so many Muslims in government that Muslims will be the leaders in America.

When former President Barack Obama was running for President, he used a logo with the letter O coming up over the horizon. The O symbolized the rising sun and a new day. It was believed that this seal was created to fulfill an Islamic prophecy found in the Hadith: "The hour will not come [judgment day] until the sun rises from the west. When it rises and the people see it, all of them will believe...."

It was suggested that this emblem was a cryptic message to Muslims in America and around the world that a new day had come and the "light of Islam" would be spread in the west by Obama.

If American chooses an anti-Israel leader, such leadership would deny military support or intervention to defend Israel during the Ezekiel conflict.

2. American's Decline

According to the books of Daniel and Revelation, at the time of the end, nations will unite to form coalitions for military, political, and economic reasons. Revelation mentions the "kings of the east," the ten-nation confederacy that will join with the Antichrist. The European Union currently has twenty-seven member countries. There are fifty-five African countries in the African Union (AU). OPEC, the Organization of Petroleum Exporting Countries, currently has twelve member nations.

BRICS is a group of nations that connected for geopolitical, trade, financial, and economic reasons. The first members included Brazil, Russia, India, China, and South Africa. Other nations joined later, making this a group of eleven, with yet others expressing interest. As these coalitions united to divest from the dollar and western dominance, America began to lose influence.

There are many reasons, both nationally and globally, for the decline of the dollar. Much of it is due to the U.S. national debt that exceeds $34 trillion and our persistent budget deficits. This means more dollars in circulation, and more inflation that decreases the value of the dollar and purchasing power. Other countries are moving away from dollar-based trade. The dollar is still one of the most stable currencies, but unless we can control our debt and spending, the dollar will lose out to other currencies.

If the U.S. economy continues to decline and if inflation keeps eating away at the value of our dollar, we will be less inclined or financially able to help other countries in times of war, including Israel or other allies.

3. America's Involvement in Wars

The U.S. has been involved in some significant wars in the last century: World War I, World War II, the Korea War, the Vietnam War, the Gulf War, and the Iraq War. We have been involved in other wars peripherally, through funding or intervention. Since World War I, the United States has spent trillions dollars on military funding for wars and global conflicts, which is more than any other country. As more Americans become aware of the financial condition of the country, and as more are suffering from the effects of the dollar's decline, many are saying enough is enough, and that we should let each country fight their own battles.

4. Natural Disasters

It is no secret that there is a strong potential for America to experience severe natural disasters, including earthquakes, tsunamis, hurricanes, and floods that could cost so much, it would bankrupt entire cities and governments. The high cost of recovery would cause Americans to focus on their own woes, and there would be no interest in supporting an ally in a foreign war.

Any combination of the above could explain why Israel might not have military support or assistance from the West, and specifically the United States. This brings us back to the original question and the statements God made to the prophet Ezekiel. The Almighty makes it clear that He will be the reason that Israel defeats their invaders. The "young lions" might appear to be restraining their involvement, because God alone intends to be glorified at the conclusion of this war:

> *"Indeed all the people of the land will be burying, and they will gain renown for it on the day that I am glorified," says the Lord God."*
>
> – Ezekiel 39:13 (NKJV)

Notice how many times God speaks of His intervention. The Lord declared, "I will turn you around..." (Ezek. 38:4); "I will bring you against My land, that the heathen may know Me..." (Ezek. 38:16); "I will call for a sword against you through all My mountains..." (Ezek. 38:21); "I will plead against him (Gog) with pestilence and blood, and I will rain upon him..." (Ezek. 38:22). God said that He will turn him back, smite the bow from his hands, and give the enemies to the ravenous birds and beasts of the field to be devoured" (Ezek. 39:2-4).

God gives the reasons why He alone is involved:

> *"Thus I will magnify Myself and sanctify Myself, and I will be known in the eyes of many nations. Then they shall know that I am the LORD."*
>
> – Ezekiel 38:23 (NKJV)

> *"I will set My glory among the nations; all the nations shall see*

My judgment which I have executed, and My hand which I have laid on them. So the house of Israel shall know that I am the Lord their God from that day forward"

– Ezekiel 39:21-23 (NKJV)

These predictions that God alone will receive the glory carry a hint that He does not intend for any supporting nation to assist Israel in this war. The nations will know that God and God alone was responsible. He alone will receive all glory, so that the nations will know that Israel's God is great.

CHAPTER 22

FIVE WAYS A NATION CAN DELAY JUDGMENT AND KEEP GOD'S FAVOR

We often hear it said that the judgment of God is coming. Divine judgment is when God sees the actions of men and nations, weighs those actions against His Word, and determines the fate of the person or nation involved in the wicked activity. In the Old Testament, there could be a personal, regional, or national chastisement or judgment released as a form of divine retribution. The judgments could include an invasion by other nations, drought, famine, pestilence, locusts, plagues, or death of cattle and other animals.

Often overlooked is that, at times, God will prepare a judgment, but through repentance He is willing to delay His vengeance. Isaiah rebuked a careless King Hezekiah for exposing the hidden gold and silver treasures to the curious eyes of visiting Babylonians. He predicted that, in the future, the Babylonians would invade Jerusalem and plunder every single item. Nothing would be left. Hezekiah was informed that God would spare him from the Babylonian invaders, but his future descendants would see the burning of Jerusalem and be forced into Babylonian captivity. This happened as the prophet warned.

The Babylonians invaded Judah, with the final destruction happening in 586 BC. Judgment was delayed until future generations.

Every nation risks the danger of following the path of ancient empires whose land mass still exists, but whose power and influence have long ceased. Their splendor and success are recalled in university textbooks and occasional documentaries. If we hope to learn from past empires and biblical narratives to gain or maintain God's favor, we should focus on the principles and commands He laid out for us in scripture.

1. Seek Righteousness

Righteousness exalts a nation, but sin is a reproach (shame, disgrace) to any people (Prov. 14:34). The Hebrew word that is used throughout the Old Testament for righteousness is *tsedaqah,* and the Greek word used throughout the New Testament is *dikaiosune*. Both refer to doing what is right according to God's standards. The Greek word also refers to being in proper relationship with God.

Of course, not everybody in each nation is seeking to be in proper relationship with God, or at least not the God that Christians serve. But citizens and leaders of every nation need a *righteous* standard to follow for the good of themselves and their nation, and the proper righteous standard is laid out by God in the Holy Bible. His Word is truth.

When people are allowed to do whatever is right in their own eyes (Judges 17:6), and when there is no righteous leadership or set of rules that people must follow, it is inevitable that conflict, chaos, and violence will follow. In America, we watch the effects of lawlessness in cities across the nation every day, to the point that people don't want to visit those cities for fear they will become a crime victim.

Consider this example of the negative effects that unrighteous leadership can have on a nation. For decades leading up to 2015, the courts and Congress passed laws that affirmed the biblical covenant of marriage between a man and a woman. This was fought back and forth in the courts for decades. Eventually, all the state legislation and various court rulings led the Supreme Court on June 26, 2015 to strike down all state bans on same-sex marriage. Regardless of what the residents of a particular state believed about the matter, they were now forced to honor licenses for same-sex marriages.

Across the country, gay couples assured us that all they wanted was to get married so they could receive the legal benefits of marriage, such as passing on assets and visiting each other in the hospital. Many Christians empathetically and ignorantly went along with it. But something happened when the highest court in the land passed a law that violated God's covenant of marriage. It opened a door for increased demonic activity that, ten years later, has caused enormous societal problems.

Right away we witnessed lawsuits against private businesses for refusing to provide services for same-sex marriage ceremonies. Christians were intentionally targeted through the legal system by people who were determined to make them pay because of their beliefs. Then we watched as segments of society have demanded that we accept drag queen story hour for children. We have watched as parents allow drag queens to entertain small children in a manner that is so perverted, it was once allowed only behind closed doors in an adult night club. We have watched the unfolding of transgenderism and told that we are bigoted and transphobic if we don't accept it as normal behavior. Court battles are being waged over the right for a young child to be given puberty blockers under the pretense of being transitioned to the opposite gender, even to the point of having their body parts removed or disfigured.

Where does this end? Will same-sex marriage become another Roe

v. Wade for our culture? Will we eventually see it overturned by the Supreme Court and sent back to the states to make their own individual laws?

Applying God's biblical standards to our lives and our government exalts and lifts up a nation. Prioritizing God's kingdom and His righteousness plays a critical role in setting a strong foundation for a nation to be blessed. Even the unrighteous among us will be blessed by righteous leadership, which the Bible tells us in Proverbs 29:2: "When the righteous are in authority, the people rejoice; But when a wicked man rules, the people groan."

2. Confront the shedding of innocent blood

Conservative Christians typically think of the shedding of innocent blood in terms of abortion only, but any deadly violence against those who are innocent is the shedding of innocent blood. When a nation legalizes abortion, as the United States did in 1973, it is unavoidable that the subsequent killing of tens of millions of unborn babies will release a spirit of murder over the nation. An unchecked spirit of murder leads to violence in the home and on the streets. People lament the increase in violent crime, never connecting it to the legalization of abortion.

Proponents of abortion didn't stop with first trimester legalization. They pushed for the removal of all gestational restrictions, and the government voted to spend taxpayer money to fund abortions. From there, abortion providers moved to selling organs and body parts of aborted babies to fill their coffers with even more money. Thankfully, the current U.S. administration issued an executive order to stop federal funding of abortion, and Congress needs to codify that into law. In no way, shape, or form should federal or state governments be funding abortion.

Five Ways a Nation Can Delay Judgment and Keep God's Favor

In the United States in 2022, the Supreme Court overturned the 1973 Roe vs. Wade court decision that legalized abortion nationally. This reversal did not outlaw abortion; it meant that individual states were now responsible for setting their own regulations.

The states wasted no time codifying abortion laws. According to the state-by-state map provided by *The Hill*, fourteen states have a near total ban on abortion, while many other states have extremely liberal abortion laws. Seven states allow abortion with no gestational limitations, meaning any point up to the time of birth. Other states allow abortion in the 20-plus week range that varies by state, while some use "up to fetal viability" language. A few states have stricter limitations, such as a six-week heartbeat law, while some states tried to strictly limit or outlaw abortions and had their bans or restrictions blocked by a judge.

If you want your state or nation to live under a self-imposed curse, one of the sure ways to do that is to legalize the shedding of innocent blood. One of the seven abominations that God hates includes hands that shed innocent blood (Prov. 6:17). God made it clear in scripture that the shedding of innocent blood brings a curse. When Cain killed Abel, God said that Abel's blood was crying out to Him from the ground. God told Cain that his action had caused him to be cursed from the earth (Gen. 4:10-11). In Numbers 35:33, God warned the people not to pollute the land with innocent blood, and if they did, justice and judgment must follow. In the New Testament, Jesus warned the people about the curse upon Jerusalem for all their shedding of innocent blood (Matt. 23:35-38).

Children are a heritage of the Lord (Psalm 127:3). Every child who is conceived deserves the opportunity to enter the world and fulfill the purpose God planned for them on the earth. Civil societies must mete out appropriate judgment to those who commit murder against the innocent.

It is shocking to observe the complete lack of regard for human life that some people exhibit. These same people will viciously target anybody who stands up for life. When a nation, a state, or an individual refuses to stop shedding innocent blood, they cannot expect to be blessed.

3. Turn from idolatry

The first commandment that God gave in Exodus 20:3 was, "You shall have no other gods before Me." When the Israelites lived in Egypt for hundreds of years, they were surrounded by false gods. The Egyptians worshipped a plethora of gods that represented just about everything, especially nature and fertility. God warned His people to worship no god but Him, yet the idolatry was so ingrained in their lives, they built a golden calf and worshipped it while Moses was on Mount Sinai receiving the commandments from God (Exodus 32).

God threatened to kill every one of them, but Moses interceded on their behalf. When Moses came off the mountain and saw what the people were doing, he was enraged. The great sin that the idol worshippers brought upon the people resulted in the deaths of three thousand men.

Today most people don't create and worship idols made from stone or clay. Modern idols take a different form—electronics, entertainment, or a selfish desire for attention and fame at any cost. Some people worship themselves, which we observe on various internet and social media platforms, where people are willing to embarrass and shame themselves by posting nonsense on the forever internet. They'll do or say anything for followers, clicks, and cash. Greed and worship of self has become an epidemic.

People have quickly become addicted to modern forms of idolatry. If more of your time and attention is focused on idolatrous addictions than on developing your relationship with Christ, advancing His

Kingdom, and spending time with your family, you might be guilty of idolatry. Each person should honestly examine their lives and habits to see what or whom they have placed above the position of God Almighty.

4. Restore just balances

Proverbs 11:1 warns, "A false balance is an abomination to the Lord; but a just weight is his delight." In ancient times, greedy and dishonest men would cheat in commerce by manipulating the weights on their scales. The result would be that the customer received less of the product than they actually paid for.

This speaks to integrity, honesty, and fairness. Societies around the world need those traits in their government, economic, and judicial systems. Justice is as much a part of the character of God as mercy and righteousness. A society where there is no fair justice, integrity, mercy, and righteousness cannot flourish.

> "He has shown you, O man, what is good; and what does the Lord require of you but to do justly, to love mercy, and to walk humbly with your God?"
>
> – MICAH 6:8 NKJV

> "To do righteousness and justice is more acceptable to the LORD than sacrifice."
>
> – PROVERBS 21:3 (NKJV)

> "But let justice run down like water, And righteousness like a mighty stream."
>
> – AMOS 5:24 (NKJV)

In recent decades, the United States has witnessed a two-tiered justice system, especially among government officials and judges, where innocent people have been falsely accused and often sent to jail, while the guilty and those accusing the innocent have remained free. All the while, those dealing unjustly tell us that "nobody is above the law." The year 2025 has brought such corruption to light in ways we have never seen before.

We also must consider how mercy and justice applies to the widows, orphans, strangers, and oppressed among us.

> *"Thus says the LORD, Do justice and righteousness, and deliver the one who has been robbed from the power of his oppressor. Also do not mistreat or do violence to the stranger, the orphan, or the widow; and do not shed innocent blood in this place."*
>
> – JEREMIAH 22:3 (NKJV)

In biblical times, when a husband died and there were no sons to care for their mother, the widow was left with nothing and nobody to care for her. This could leave her destitute. The same situation applied to orphans, called "the fatherless" in scripture. With no family alive to care for them, the orphan was left vulnerable and destitute.

In the Torah, the Hebrew people were given a harvest law, the law of gleaning. They were to leave a certain area of their grain fields and vineyards untouched so that the poor and stranger among them would have food provisions.

Today, most wealthy countries have government resources and organizations in their communities to provide for the poor and needy. Churches often help as well. Our ministry assists specific orphanages in other countries, and we help legitimate ministries that we know well, here and abroad, with their food and programs for the poor.

I am aware that there are shysters who take advantage of people and pretend that they need help when they do not. Our ministry has had to deal with crooks taking on our identity and begging people to support a project, such as a non-existent orphanage that they falsely claim we support. Scammers target naïve people by claiming to be raising money for a worthy and heart-wrenching project, when in fact the money is being used to fund their own living expenses.

The Bible rebukes people who are able to work but don't because they are lazy, calling them sloths and sluggards, and warning that their laziness will cause poverty. The Apostle Paul said that they did not eat anybody's bread free of charge, but they worked, so as not to be a burden to anybody. He said that if anyone would not work, neither should they eat (2 Thess. 3:8, 10). The sluggard makes excuses for why he cannot work, such as we see in Proverbs 22:13: There's a lion outside, and I'll be killed in the streets!

There is no doubt that some of the people holding "please help, need money" signs are misusing the money they are given. There is, however, a blessing for those who help the truly poor and needy. Proverbs 19:17 tells us that whoever is generous to the poor lends to the Lord, and He will repay him for his deed.

There are also biblical rules for how to treat the strangers who live among us. In the Torah, God reminded Israel to respect the stranger among them and not to abuse them, reminding His people that they too were once strangers and slaves in Egypt. In Leviticus 24:22, they were told to apply the same laws to the stranger as they did to themselves—one ordinance for everybody. The strangers were to be free from working on the Sabbath (Exod. 20:10). The Hebrews were not to oppress or exploit a stranger living among them (Exod. 23:9). The stranger was expected to respect moral and ceremonial laws, and the stranger should be allowed to bring a sacrifice and participate in worship with God's people (Num. 15).

These rules can be applied in a modern context to immigrants as well, as they are strangers in the country. Immigration has become a highly volatile and sensitive issue over the last few years, after an open border policy allowed tens of millions of unvetted people to freely enter the country. Europe experienced this in 2015 when around 1.3 million unvetted migrants arrived by boat and entered Germany, Sweden, France, and the UK. Most were from Middle Eastern Islamic countries and the majority were young men. While they were initially welcomed, the influx created many social, economic, and political problems, as citizens have been faced with increased levels of crime, a reduction of resources for the citizens of those countries, and political upheaval.

The world has seen firsthand that open borders allow dangerous people into the country, many of whom are fleeing their home countries to avoid justice for crimes they committed. The U.S. has seen an influx that includes drug dealers and cartel members, human traffickers, potential terrorists, and violent gang members. Every citizen of every nation ought to agree that dangerous criminals should not be welcomed into the country. Every country has laws that govern immigration, and the laws need to be enforced to maintain security for their own citizens.

Other immigrants come to escape persecution or with the hope of making a better life for themselves and their children. This is one reason why immigration, and in particular illegal entry into a country, is such a hot button issue. Once laws have been broken for entry, countries must determine how to deal with the subsequent security and economic issues as they enforce laws and do so using both justice and mercy.

We are biblically told to treat strangers with respect and not to abuse them physically or economically. None should be victimized and taken advantage of through illegal behaviors such as trafficking or unjust wages.

A nation must ensure that their laws are obeyed and enforced, so that lawlessness does not reign. No nation is prepared to handle a flood of millions of people crossing their borders on the scale that we have witnessed globally in the last decade. Those who want to come for a better life should follow the legal process set out by the nation they hope to enter, and then they should work toward becoming a productive citizen of the country they now call home.

5. Pray for your nation and pray for Israel

One thing is vital to the success of any nation, and that is prayer. We should lift our leaders up and pray for them to have God's divine wisdom as they make decisions.

> "Therefore I exhort first of all that supplications, prayers, intercessions, and giving of thanks be made for all men, for kings and all who are in authority, that we may lead a quiet and peaceable life in all godliness and reverence. For this is good and acceptable in the sight of God our Savior."
>
> – 1 Tim. 2:1-2 (NKJV)

> "If My people who are called by My name will humble themselves, and pray and seek My face, and turn from their wicked ways, then I will hear from heaven, and will forgive their sin and heal their land."
>
> – 2 Chronicles 7:14 (NKJV)

Our prayers and repentance have the power to bring peace, security, and healing to a nation.

With respect to Israel, I also take literally the biblical promise that God spoke over Abraham, "I will bless those who bless you, and I will curse him who cures you" (Gen. 12:3). God promised that if Israel would walk in obedience to His will and follow His commandments, no person or nation would be able to remove God's favor from them. In Numbers 23, the Moabite king named Balak paid a seer named Balaam to curse Israel's massive encampment that was set up in the plains of Moab. Balaam attempted to curse them, but instead he blessed them. In Numbers 23:8, Balaam confessed, "How shall I curse whom God has not cursed? And how shall I denounce whom the LORD has not denounced?" Balaam blessed Israel three times (Num. 24:10). The message in this narrative is that "it is impossible to curse what God has blessed."

I have been involved in fundraising directed toward various projects in Israel. For years, our ministry has financially supported the needs of Arab Christians and families in Bethlehem, Jerusalem, and Nazareth, as we have provided food, medicine, and jobs during times when they were in dire need of assistance. Other times, our ministry has assisted in providing items such as fire and chemical protective shoes, clothing, and equipment for Israel to defend their villages.

Since the mid-1980s, I have organized tours to the Holy Land. Each tourist supports eleven different people in the hotel and hospitality industry. These early trips inspired me to study and later present prophetic insight, revealing firsthand through slides of actual locations in Israel, how ancient prophecies are now being fulfilled. Blessings began to flow in our direction, both personally and in the ministry, when we started blessing people in Israel.

Up to this point, the United States has been a supporter of Israel since its establishment in 1948. Many still believe, and the Bible tells us, that if we continue to stand with Israel, we connect to the covenant favor of God. Supporting Israel does not mean that you must agree with every government decision. People in the U.S. disagree and fight over every decision made by their *own* government, yet at the end of the day, most stand with and support America. The command to bless Israel does not say, "You must agree with every government decision." Yet, that is how some people interpret the biblical command, and they turn against the nation because they don't like a government decision.

I was told this story about a time when Bill Clinton was governor of Arkansas. He lost an election, which upset him quite a bit. His pastor told him that he would one day become president of the United States, at a time when Israel needed a friend. He warned Clinton that if he ever turned against Israel, God would turn against him. Clinton later addressed the Knesset in Israel, telling them that the trip had restored his faith.

During Clinton's administration, he began to discuss a two state solution, which refers to carving out parts of Israel for a separate Palestinian state. As splitting the land was discussed and negotiations were conducted behind closed doors, something happened. A Jewish woman was told by a young Jewish intern named Monica that she had been in a relationship with Bill Clinton. The information was leaked publicly and became worldwide news. Of course, this was Clinton's own making, and it caused him a great deal of trouble.

Some of my greatest friends are from Israel, and they include Arabs, Christians, and Jews. These are the people living together in the Holy Land. This land was given to the descendants of Abraham through Isaac and Jacob, and it is where God said multiple times that He put His name. This land is where the Messiah will return to rule, and when He sets up His throne in Jerusalem, all nations will come there to worship during the Feast of Tabernacles.

CHAPTER 23

IN CONCLUSION

I believe we are the "trigger generation." We are seeing many hints, clues, and prophetic patterns and predictions emerge, as no other generation in the past 1,900 years has experienced. Here is a summary of the coming triggers.

1. The America Triggers

Believers in the United States often view prophetic events with a focus on the ways those events impact our country, at times ignoring the fact that the United States represents only 4.3 percent of the entire world's population. Much of prophecy is centered in the Middle East, and it specifically involves Israel. Over the last century, the United States involvement in world affairs has been significant, but several factors could change this.

One factor would be severe economic decline. Many things could cause this, not the least of which is our suffocating national debt and the lack of congressional desire to control spending.

Another factor in the decline of our position and influence would be if we experienced a significant number of severe natural disasters. Fault lines along the Pacific Coast threaten the west coast with earthquakes and tsunamis. An earthquake fault line runs down the center of the country, and people are sometimes surprised to feel an earthquake in an outlying area. We have been told that a Yellowstone volcano could erupt. We have seen an increase in damaging floods, fires, hurricanes, and tornadoes. All are part of the end-time predictions (Luke 21:25; Matt. 24:7). Devastating natural disasters always impact the economy, food supplies, utilities, and transportation. As birth pains intensify, we likely will experience trigger events that force us to focus only on our own nation and citizens.

The third factor contributing to our downfall could be nationwide civil unrest. Almost every week, we see reports of out-of-control mobs of youth, especially in large cities, wreaking havoc on businesses and residents. In some cities, businesses that are vital to the community are shutting their doors because of robberies and violence. Racial division, gang activity, violence, and illegal drugs are just a few of the exploding dangers in America's cities.

Regardless of the causes, a power shift will one day come where the west will decline, and economic and governmental authority will shift to the east. Let's also not forget the single event that will change the position of America immediately and dramatically—the sudden catching away of the bride of Christ. This event will immediately create global chaos, and "peace will be taken from the earth" (Rev. 6:4).

2. The Trigger of Prophetic Wars

Christ warned of wars and rumors of wars, and of the conflict of nation rising against nation and kingdom against kingdom (Matt. 24:6-7). Wars and modern weapons have the capability to trigger other prophetic indicators of the end of the age, such as famine, war and widespread death. Many readers are old enough to have witnessed an increasing number of wars that have impacted nations and economies, wars that have changed entire boundaries and leadership of nations throughout the world.

Outside of the final Battle of Armageddon, the most significant war of Bible prophecy will be the War of Gog of Magog, directed by the future Islamic coalition. This war will be the turning point that triggers treaties and changes in the balance of power. This war will be a sign to the nations that Israel's God has the power to protect His nation.

That leads to the mother of all battles, the Battle of Armageddon. Daniel noted that "The end of it shall be with a flood, and until the end of the war desolations are determined" (Dan. 9:26). John overheard people in the Great Tribulation ask, "Who is like the beast? Who is able to make war with him?" (Rev. 13:4). The Antichrist system is one that wages war (Rev. 11:7; 12:17; 13:7; 17:14). There will be a short season of peace and safety before sudden destruction strikes the earth (1 Thess. 5:3).

3. Israel — The Time Clock of End-Time Prophecy

It is disturbing to hear those claiming to be Christians argue against supporting Israel. These biblically illiterate people claim that the modern state of Israel has no prophetic or biblical significance to the time of the end. This ideology is called "replacement theology," which teaches that the church has *replaced* Israel, and that Christians have *replaced* the Jewish people as God's chosen people. Even the Apostle Paul noted that the church is not replacing Israel; we are the wild olive tree that was *grafted into* the covenant promises made to Abraham, and we are not to become arrogant about it. We don't support the root of the olive tree; the root supports us (Romans 11:17-18).

That one chapter in the New Testament, Romans 11, destroys the basis of replacement theology. The Jews are the natural olive tree and the Gentiles are the wild olive tree. God grafted the Gentiles into the tree of Israel, and at the time of the end, He will *graft the natural branch back into the tree.* Paul warned the Gentiles not to be ignorant of this mystery, as he noted that, "Blindness in part has happened to Israel until the fullness of the Gentiles has come in" (Rom. 11:25). He continued by saying, "And so all Israel shall be saved" (Rom. 11:26). Zechariah 13:6 notes that Christ will be asked, "What are those wounds in your hands?" And He will reply, "I was wounded in the house of my friends."

In the future, Israel will experience the time of Jacob's trouble (Jer. 30:7), when they will endure the Great Tribulation as Satan makes one final attempt to eradicate the natural seed of Abraham. However, God will bring one-third of His people through the fire and refine them as silver (Zech. 13:9). They will call on His name, and He will hear them; and they shall say, "The LORD is my God."

In the book of Revelation, the church is addressed in chapters 2 and 3. From chapters 4 through 19, the focus in on the tribulation judgment, the two witnesses (Rev. 11), the rise of the Antichrist and False Prophet (Rev. 13), the sealing and catching up of 144,000 Jewish men (Rev. 7 and 14), and events occurring with the saints in heaven. When the church is removed from the earth, God's focus will be the preservation and salvation of Israel.

Those who believe in replacement theology have a misunderstanding and lopsided view of the entire picture of that biblically prophetic word.

4. The Formation of the Beast Kingdom

In Daniel and Revelation, both Daniel and John described the Antichrist as a "beast" (Daniel 7:7; Revelation 11:7; 13:1-17, and 17:3-17). In Revelation, the Greek word for beast is *therion,* which describes a dangerous, fiendish wild beast. The word is used to identify the Antichrist, and it reveals the powerful and deadly nature of this future world dictator. Paul wrote that the man of sin (Antichrist) would be revealed in "his time," when the restrainer who resists the rise of lawlessness is taken out of the way (2 Thess. 2:7-8).

In Conclusion

It is my opinion that, when the Islamic coalition is defeated on the mountains of Israel, leaving one-sixth of the armies remaining, this will open the door for the Daniel 9:27 treaty to be signed by Israel and many nations. This will call for a new Islamic leadership and a reorganization and unification of the Islamic nations under one banner. That war will trigger a temporary peace which will eventually be broken and lead to the Armageddon military campaign (Rev. 16:16).

Numerous events will merge coalitions, nations, and religions, while at the same time cause division in nations and religions. This is part of the process.

Your most important assignment before that time is to enter into a redemptive covenant with Christ, follow the rules of heaven, and gain eternal life. Arm yourself with God's word. Study prophecy for both your personal understanding and to share these truths with those who are not prepared to meet Christ and stand before Him at the judgment.

Scan this code to view the images and maps referenced in this book.

https://perrystone.org/bk39maps

Expose the Sequence of Satanic Attacks Against You and Your Family

BK-038 | $20

ORDER ONLINE AT PERRYSTONE.ORG
OR CALL (423) 478.3456

Visions of Those Things Which Were, and Those Things Which are to Come

BK-032 | $20

ORDER ONLINE AT PERRYSTONE.ORG

OR CALL (423) 478.3456

A MUST READ FOR EVERY PATRIOTIC-LOVING AMERICAN

BK-030 | $20

ORDER ONLINE AT PERRYSTONE.ORG

OR CALL (423) 478.3456